Asking and Listening

Asking and Listening

Ethnography as Personal Adaptation

Paul Bohannan
Dirk van der Elst

WAVELAND
PRESS, INC.

Prospect Heights, Illinois

For information about this book, write or call:
  Waveland Press, Inc.
  P.O. Box 400
  Prospect Heights, Illinois 60070
  (847) 634-0081

Contents

Four Notes

1. This short book was written to stimulate discussion, not to convert you to any particular view. We expect both students and teachers to disagree with some of it, but every subject we mention here needs wide discussion.

2. This book is about ethnography, which means the descriptions of various cultures by which people live. Elsewhere you may run across the term "ethnology." That is the theory of how to understand the interlinking of many ethnographies—and a different subject.

3. "I" in this book refers to Bohannan. "We" means both of us.

4. Karla Poewe, Estellie Smith, and Mari Womack read this book critically. All of them made suggestions, for which we are grateful. The flaws, of course, remain ours, not theirs.

Part I

Alien Beings
with
Human Faces

Like all animals, human beings are both drawn to and afraid of strangers, because even though strangers are in many ways like ourselves, they act and appear different.

Chapter One

The Others

People have "always" known that there were "Others" living just beyond their territories: human beings who spoke in strange tongues and practiced unusual customs. People have "always" been interested in those Others. Knowing that the strangers were not animals or spirit beings but humans like themselves encouraged a certain guardedness: if those not-too-distant neighbors are no better than we are, they may be capable of who knows what! But early humans lived in small, isolated bands; people saw new faces relatively seldom, and that did make strangers a novelty.

Today, when communication can proceed at the speed of light and travel can carry us beyond the speed of sound, the need to understand the Other—all the Others—takes on a new immediacy. Novelty is as important as ever, but security is also a crucial consideration because strangers often prove dangerous—and today they are no longer merely at the gate; the very gate has ceased to exist. Modern population densities make strangers of us all, so we are all in this together. One of the gravest problems for the twenty-first century is how we cope with the fears that cluster around ethnicity, the idea that keeps separating us from the Others while technology keeps bringing us all together.

The problem is not exactly new. People have been aware of it for millennia. Well over two thousand years ago, the Roman poet and playwright Terence wrote, "Nothing human is alien to me." Terence was born in Carthage, in North Africa, but taken to Rome as a slave. There the senator who was his master educated him and ultimately set him free. By then, Romans had ceased to be alien to him. The story goes that after the production of his last play, Terence (still a young man at the time) took a trip "to the East" from which he never returned; perhaps he found a place he liked better than either Carthage or Rome.

In modern urban existence, aliens are all around us—in perception if not in reality: the very meaning of the word "alien" now even includes "creatures from outer space." We constantly encounter people who seem outlandish to us either culturally or psychologically (many of us do not bother to distinguish). We minimize contact with them on general principle.

3

We are, however, still as clear about distinguishing Us and Not-Us as we ever were. The behavior of foreigners is always "alien." But so may be that of your neighbors down the street. Your own grandparents probably seem at least a little alien, and if you are in the first generation of your line to be born in North America, they almost certainly will be. And *do* expect your own children to become aliens—at least for a few years.

In fact, all sorts of "things human" are alien to every one of us, every day.

Still, if you take Terence's statement as a goal, it makes as much sense as ever. The less of human behavior that is foreign to you, the fuller the life you can lead. The goal is to be able to say truthfully in your old age, "*Almost* nothing human is alien to me."

As global culture spreads around the world, people become increasingly aware that we are all in this together because we are all parts of the human species. Disciplines old and new are approaching this realization with ideas like "multiculturalism." Each perspective brings different tools to its examination. Literature looks at multicultural situations from the standpoint of art. Ethnic studies programs look at them primarily from the viewpoint of power. There are many positions from which to look at the problems associated with ethnicity, and all are legitimate.

The oldest organized approach is found in anthropology. Anthropologists invented what we call "ethnography," which is its label for "an orderly description of people with exotic lifeways"—exotic, that is, to the reader: there are a growing number of ethnographers reporting on their own societies. The "ethno" comes from the same root as "ethnic": the "other" people.

Which brings us to the point of this book.

As the world you live in becomes more accessible, more and more of the people you deal with are Others. If you live long enough, you'll realize that *everybody* is "Other." The way Others act and think may be almost incomprehensible—until you begin to understand something about what people take for granted about life, the universe, and their selves. We each have unexamined assumptions about everything that matters to us, and though we may agree about what is important, we may totally disagree about what these important things require of society and the individual.

So how can you overcome that limitation on your capacity to comprehend and interact with your fellow human beings for fun and profit?

Ethnography, the approach which anthropologists pioneered, is no longer "merely" the description of the lifeways of exotic and faraway folk; it is now both a vast and growing reference library, and a busy enterprise for making people from different cultures comprehensible to each other. Its subject matter ranges from the familiar to the mind-boggling.

Our aim is to convince you that the more ethnography you understand, the greater the range of alternatives you will have for choosing and running your life. After all, if you don't know at least one alternative, you don't *have* a choice.

You may well, in the long run, opt for the cultural ways you were taught when you were growing up—but if so, it should be because broad experience (both vicarious and direct) has shown you their superiority. The values and customs of your parental culture may sometimes seem old-fashioned. But they *have* had time to adapt to a great range of circumstances—far more time than you have. Moreover, not every new alternative is a good one: AIDS, teen-age pregnancy, addiction, and the hopelessness of gang life all prove that hormones and peer pressure may not always be the best guides to a good life.

But it is also true that the fact of its being old does not make any tradition a good one. If you have understood both these factors and taken heed accordingly—if you comprehend the costs as well as the benefits of the alternatives implicit in other cultures, and if they make you still want to reject some of your old ways—then trust yourself. You will have discovered your own most rewarding version of being human. You'll have met the Others, and they'll no longer be quite so alien.

Moreover, learning something about them does not mean you have to join them. You can expand the dimensions within which you live without abandoning who you are. You now know that Others aren't doing it that way because they are benighted or ignorant—they do it because they think their way is a good way to do it.

A couple of points need to be made here. As you learn about Others from an ethnography, you may react emotionally to this translation of an alien lifeway into the language you read. You may find it charming and want instantly to go there. But more likely you will find some of it utterly revolting. That's okay: it takes strong emotional reactions to get people connected with strange ideas. But as you think about it, you must realize that *it* isn't revolt*ing*; it is *you* who are revolt*ed*. Where did you learn to be revolted by that?

We are not denying that some behavior is abhorrent to all sane human beings. We all know that some people do things that they themselves consider sickening—either because they can't figure out a nonrepugnant way to do them or else because they have been taught that some god or politician or enemy *demands* this "revolting" behavior. But most of what you find revolting is so because you *learned* to be revolted by it.

The Tiv of central Nigeria are revolted when their neighbors eat monkeys and dogs, which the Tiv consider akin to cannibalism. North Americans feel something similar about the European habit of eating horse meat.

Your reaction to ethnographic facts will tell you, if you let it, not merely how you feel about the way these Others live, but how you feel about how *you yourself* live. The word "feel," by the way, is treacherous enough that we should examine it. Scientists will tell you that feelings have no place in science. They are right. However, anthropologists and scientists are human. If they are alive (and most of the ones who ever lived are alive today) they have feelings whether they like it or not. If you try to banish your feelings, you will fail. You cannot banish genuine hunger by declaring that you are not hungry. Just so, you cannot banish feelings by claiming that you don't have them or that you are excluding them. The purpose of your feelings is to help you figure yourself out. The better you can do that, the better you can figure out everything else. Feelings are not the stuff of science, but they *are* the stuff of getting your act together. Of course, if your feelings are provincial—meaning "without an awareness of alternatives"—they can mislead you.

Knowing about alien people is not dangerous. It won't send you off the deep end. It won't even push you over if you are already teetering. More likely it will help pull you back. For example, in 1948, when Alfred Kinsey was the first to study and report on the sexual activity of what he called "the human male" (he meant the Midwestern, middle-class North American male), whole generations of men sighed in relief to learn that they were not unusual or distorted or perverted. The kind of knowledge—ethnographic knowledge—that Kinsey gave us was called "filth" by the squeamish who declared that it was wrong or sinful for anybody to know stuff like that. And, by the way, Congress in the late 1990s is still blocking funds for the National Institutes of Health to discover what the sexual practices of people in the United States actually are *today.*

So go ahead, ask yourself how you *feel* about those data on alien peoples? Even more important, how do you really *feel* about your own culture? And most important of all, because you are human, how do you feel about *acting* human? How do you feel about the ways you were taught to do things—ways that are, no matter how "good" you find them, good enough only until you find better ones?

You will soon find that knowing two or more cultures is like having two eyes: it gives you something resembling binocular vision. And knowing another culture gives you a place to stand while you take a good look at the one you were born into.

Learning some ethnography means that you find out something about how "the other half" lives. But of even greater personal importance, it also means that you learn something about the way *you yourself* live. You cannot think about or talk about *their* way without contrasting it with your own way—and that leads to better understanding of your own world. You can fathom alternatives and make choices purposefully. Learning some ethnography thus expands your options. Another word for that is "education."

Chapter Two

Becoming You

As you grow up, you adjust to your environment, which is mainly the culture of the people around you. As you make choices in that environment, you become who you are. That process may blind you to the lives of people who faced different alternatives. This blindness, called "ethnocentrism," can become a grave disadvantage because it so limits your ability to adapt.

If you had been brought up in another part of the world, speaking a different language in a different culture, would you be the same person?

The answer is Yes—and No. Because your genes would be the same, so would your innate potential. But human potential can only develop in response to an environment. Everywhere, the human environment is dominated by culture. You can learn whatever is available in your surroundings (human beings are capable of learning all their lives), but unfortunately you cannot learn anything that is not there. So if you were raised in a different culture, there would be differences in the results, in who and what you are.

Culture turns you into a fully-human being. But there is a catch: at the same time that your culture makes you human, it makes you provincial. You become human *your* way. Everybody else is human in a slightly—or perhaps immensely—different fashion. So as your culture defines you, it mentally imprisons you.

But culture also liberates you. It allows you to be more than an animal, for all that you never cease to be one. It provides you with the tools you need to deal with other people and to make your living; when you consider the world around you, you reason from the premises—the unquestioned assumptions— which your culture impressed upon you.

Your culture provides the perspective from which you view the world. That perspective works like a distorting mirror. While you acquired your culture, you learned to see everything in terms of the particular distortions it imposes on "reality." In fact, every perceived reality is a cultural fabrication, so

7

yours is necessarily different from the realities taken for granted by people with other cultures.

That may be the most difficult trick of all to see through, because the distortion is not evident as long as you always look into that one mirror. Having only one looking glass, you never discover that you are a prisoner of its refraction. The only way to recognize that is to look into a different mirror, one which deforms reality in another way. Only then can you see that you've had a point of view all along.

Ethnography provides every person who will use it with many additional mirrors. It lets you discover how the mirror you looked in as you grew up slanted your view of things. If you have several mirrors, each with its own distortion, you have an opportunity to triangulate on actuality—to look at it from several points of view.

If you learn some ethnography, you can use not only your own views but those of other cultures to "test out" your perceptions. You may not be completely out of the trap of culture, but you will certainly have enlarged it. You have more options, you can make more-informed choices. You are more in control of your life than you were before. Knowing some ethnography gives you a clarity of vision that you cannot achieve in any other way.

The condition of living with a single distorting mirror and assuming that *it* is the "reality" against which all people and deeds are to be judged, is called *ethnocentrism*. The word means "centered on your own culture's vision, distortion and all." You are being ethnocentric whenever you use the standards of your own culture to judge people who are acting on the premises of some other culture. You are a hopeless case if you continue to believe that the distortion in your own mirror is The One Reality, that everybody else has it "wrong." If culture is a prison, ethnocentrism bangs the cell door behind you.

Ethnocentrism invites social chaos when individuals, on the basis of their own ignorance, disadvantage other people. To the ethnocentric person, "they" are simply wrong. Or stupid. Or evil. The Other ceases to be a fellow human being and becomes the fall-guy. The next step ("We'll fix them for seeing it the wrong way!") is to turn the Other into a victim—and thereby turn yourself into a villain.

The real glory of ethnography—we cannot say it too often—is that by showing you how "the other half" lives, it also shows you how you yourself live. It throws your ways into a larger context. It expands your knowledge—and knowledge is the foundation of power.

One thing to beware of as you expand your knowledge: once written down, ethnographic descriptions become static. In the real world, cultural contexts change as people find what they consider better ways to do what they have to do. They can add to their culture and change their ways. In this sense, ethnography is like photography: it records a slice of time. Things that happened before the picture was taken are not to be seen, and things that happened after it was taken are also absent. But don't let this apparently static quality fool you; what people do is constantly in process. Ethnography is something like history: it describes conditions and events in another people's past at some specific time. But culture is happening *all* the time.

Gertrude Stein, an American writer who lived in Paris during the early part of the twentieth century, said it well in her peculiar way: "Things happen all the time, but history happens all the time from time to time."

Ethnography thus enlarges your grasp of what it means to be human. And that is the heartland of an education. You expect education to change your life as it enlarges your cultural context (as well, of course, as your opportunities—those may be the same thing). Ethnography helps, because it gives you a lot of examples of how universal problems have been approached and handled in a variety of settings—and incidentally, because it exposes the provinciality of your own ways. There can be comforts and rewards in aspects of provinciality, but only if you are able to select them from a larger menu—you wouldn't want the same thing for every meal.

It has taken well over a hundred years for ethnography's practitioners to learn how to get some of the distortion out of their cultural descriptions, and that job is not yet finished. Meanwhile, however, you can already learn to recognize how your own culture's way of channeling perception has imprisoned you. It may take specialized training to get a good *job*, but ethnography is what a good *education* is all about.

Chapter Three

Ethnography before
Anthropology

---

*Our earliest ethnographic facts—that is, facts about peoples who are for-
eign or even alien to the observer—are to be found in ancient travel books
and histories and in the records of the "voyages of discovery" from the fif-
teenth century through the nineteenth. These books were the "best-sellers"
of their day.*

Accounts by travelers about "Others" completely alien to themselves are
among the earliest written records. The Greek historian Herodotus, who lived
from about 484 to about 425 B.C., left us descriptions of his travels which
ranged from Aswan on the Nile in southern Egypt, north to the Danube in central Europe, and from Libya in North Africa eastward to the northern shores
of the Black Sea. The subject of his writings was a history of the wars between
Greece and Persia, but he also recorded ethnographic facts about the people he
met in his travels. He tells us about strange foods, strange family loyalties and
strange sexual customs, as well as about successions of kings, battles, special
achievements, and dirty political tricks.

Herodotus did not compile a descriptive record of any of the peoples he
encountered; he was interested only in the "strangeness" of their ways. He
believed (or sometimes disbelieved) what third parties told him and didn't
bother to check his information with other people who might have different
opinions. That sort of double-checking came much later.

Some people have, from time immemorial, adapted to strange Others by
taking up residence with those aliens and becoming one of them. Alexander the
Great (356–323 B.C.), for example, was the son of a king of Macedonia in the
backwoods of northern Greece. A military genius, he conquered most of the
"known world" of his day, and adapted skillfully to every culture he met (while
never quite abandoning his own). Alexander found the Persian institutions of
kingship and military more to his liking than those he had known before, so he

lived the latter part of his short life as if he were a Persian king. There is little new in people changing their cultural affiliation.

Some individuals can get truly immersed in encounters with the Other. Marco Polo lived from A.D. 1254 to 1324, or perhaps a little later. His father and uncle were long-distance traders from Venice, which was at that time the most powerful trading empire in the Western world. They traveled about a third of the way around the world to the court of Kublai Khan in China, which they called Cathay. When they left to go home, the Khan urged them to return.

On their second trip, the Polo brothers took seventeen-year-old Marco with them. That journey (on foot, in small boats, and on camel-back) lasted twenty-four years. When Marco returned home, Venice was engaged in a war with Genoa, and he was taken prisoner. While in a Genoese prison, Marco dictated his experiences in Cathay to another prisoner, who wrote them down in Old French (the literary language of the time) and published them.

Marco Polo's narrative is probably the most widely read travel book of all time. The Khan was interested in the many different peoples of his empire. After Marco entered his service, he traveled widely in what today are China, Tibet, Laos, and Viet Nam gathering information for the Khan about the peoples there.

Much of what we know about Kublai Khan comes from Marco Polo—other sources by and large confirm what he wrote. Marco's account of his travels is not exactly ethnography because his purpose was somewhat different. But he recorded many facts that, in a slightly different context, would have been an integral part of an ethnography. For example:

> The unlicensed intercourse of the sexes is not in general considered by these people [of Tangut] as a serious offence, and their maxim is that, if the advances are made by a female, the connexion does not constitute an offence, but it is held to be such when the proposal comes from the man. . . . The laiety take as many as thirty wives . . . according to their ability to maintain them; for they do not receive any dowry with them, but, on the contrary settle dowers upon their wives, in cattle, slaves, and money. The wife who is first married always maintains the superior rank in the family.[1]

You can still find that sort of statement, with a little more detail and modern word usage, in the reports of ethnographers today.

Christopher Columbus studied Marco Polo's book—his copy of it has margin notes written in his own hand. Indeed, when Columbus started out, his intention was to sail west (instead of riding a camel toward the east) to find the court of the Khan. As we all know, he never made it because North and South America were in the way. But Columbus left notes about the Native Americans of the islands of the Caribbean, especially the Caribs themselves. Those notes are short because Columbus was more interested in gold than he was in people—but they are there.

We have hundreds of accounts from the period of discovery that followed Columbus's voyages. Many of those accounts contain preliminary—one might almost say primitive—descriptions of peoples living in the areas being "discovered."

These accounts of voyages became best-sellers—they were the favorite reading of almost everybody during the 1600s and 1700s. Beginning in the middle 1800s, Great Britain's Hakluyt Society (named for Richard Hakluyt, who was the first professor of geography in England) brought many together into a huge collection and republished them widely.

A knowledge of strange people in strange places was essential to international commerce. As trade developed and knowledge increased, people became more and more aware of themselves as being different from the peoples they met. It would, however, be the end of the nineteenth century before any methodical exploration of these differences was launched.

Missionaries wrote about the people they tried to turn into Christians. In fact, nineteenth-century European missionaries were instrumental in the development of anthropological methods, and their letters and diaries in missionary archives are often the first trustworthy sources for the history of native life in areas of Africa, Australia, China, India, Indonesia, and the Pacific. The Berlin Mission Society, for example, required each of its missionaries to speak the language of the population he or she sought to convert, to earn the people's trust by living with as well as among them, and to learn to understand their customs and values. Other major missionary societies in Germany, Holland, Scandinavia, and elsewhere maintained similar standards.

But some missionaries from the less intellectually rigorous faiths were lax in checking their facts—they pandered to the then-prevalent European myths about the "depravity" of non-Christian "savages," apparently hoping to draw larger contributions to the missionary fund. The idea of the "savage" has always turned not so much on observed fact as on what "civilized" folk viewed as the "opposite" of themselves. A few writers still do this: in describing prehistory they start not from the known facts but rather from what, they fancy, are the opposites of the particular cultural achievements they want to celebrate.

In the 1800s, some European women went on voyages of discovery. One, Mary Kingsley, traveled through West Africa "in petticoats," as the phrase went, because in those days "decent" women never wore trousers. Her books, though organized around her adventures and woefully incomplete, nevertheless contain valuable ethnographic information. Kingsley was, by the way, among the first to understand the problems Africans were facing—and from the Africans' point of view.

Sir Richard Burton (1821–1890) (who shared nothing more than his name with the actor who twice married Elizabeth Taylor) was an adventurer of formidable intelligence who detested his native British culture and escaped it regularly to travel in strange realms. He made a precarious living writing about the places he had been, completing the first (and still one of the best) English translations of the *Arabian Nights*. He once traveled as a pilgrim to Mecca, knowing full well that if he, an infidel, had been discovered, he would have been executed. He wrote several books about the peoples of Africa. He translated the *Kama Sutra*.

After his death, Burton's widow Isabella destroyed his extensive, unpublished ethnographic notes because they contained a lot of what she considered obscene language and topics, and she wanted to assure him a sacrosanct reputation. Her act may not have been equivalent to burning the Library of Alexandria, but she deprived the world for all time of an expert's accounts of first contact with societies now lost or changed beyond recognition.

In those days, ethnography had not yet separated from travel writing. Early books of travel contain information about Other people which has proved to be accurate. None of the authors, however, had the aim of *explaining* the lifeways of the people they met. Travel writers, then as now, write about their own adventures in strange places. Sometimes these involve people of alien cultures. Travel writing remains an honorable genre, but its focus has changed as more and more tourists travel to distant sites and the "unknown" world becomes familiar.

By the 1920s, the geography of the world was pretty well known. You had to look pretty hard for adventure. Ethnography had broken off from travel writing in the late 1800s, as anthropologists were constructing ideas about culture.

The great voyages occupy an important place in the history of Western literature—something like the place that science fiction now holds. The difference is that science fiction is admittedly fabrication, whereas the old travel books presented a little fact mixed with a lot of fancy as God's Truth. However, without their example, *Gulliver's Travels*—and probably *The Lord of the Rings*—could never even have been imagined.

Note

[1] *Travels of Marco Polo*. Introduction by John Masefield (New York: Dutton, 1967), 113.

Chapter Four

The Discovery of Culture and the Discovery of Comparison

The discovery of the idea of culture, about 1870, turned ethnography into a totally new course. The reasons for the differences among peoples no longer had to be attributed to "blood," or climate, or moral disintegration.

In the 1860s, a revolution in ideas overtook both Europe and the United States. The idea of evolution was at its heart. The idea of evolution is old: it can be traced back to Roman poets like Lucretius. In the mid-1800s it showed up in the works of Herbert Spencer (1820–1903), an Englishman who wrote extensively about philosophy and society. Then in 1859, Darwin did something new and daring: his *On the Origin of Species* demonstrated how the old idea of evolution could be applied to biology.

The idea of the evolution of culture, as people like Herbert Spencer wrote about it, had not excited much antipathy. But ideas about *biological* evolution challenged religious notions about the creation of human beings. Darwinism earned the undying hostility of those fundamentalist sects that interpret the Bible literally, and not until 1997 did the Pope acknowledge that evolution and God's will are not necessarily in opposition.

Two books, both published in 1871, altered the way human differences were explained, and thereby completely changed the way people looked at the Other. Those two books—Edward Burnett Tylor's *Primitive Culture* and Lewis H. Morgan's *Systems of Consanguinity and Affinity*—put the many known facts about alien peoples into a totally new light. Incidentally, they also date the formal beginnings of cultural anthropology. Some of their ideas are outmoded now, but their organization of the facts gave us an absolutely new way to look at alien peoples.

Edward Burnett Tylor (1832–1917) was an English Quaker. Because of his faith he could not get into any English university in the 1850s—only members of the Church of England were admitted. (In today's world this would be called religious prejudice.) Tylor therefore went to work in his father's business, a prospering brass foundry. Then, in his mid-twenties, he became ill. His doctor advised rest and travel.

Tylor first went to Cuba, where he joined Henry Christie, another Quaker and a friend of his parents. Tylor and Christie took a six-month tour of Mexico. When Tylor recovered his health and returned to England, he wrote *Anahuac, or Mexico and Mexicans, Ancient and Modern*. Intellectually, that particular work didn't achieve much beyond the traditional travel book. But it cemented Tylor's interest in the native peoples of Mexico and their ancestors.

Tylor had read a lot of travel books and accounts of voyages. He began to see similarities among the various peoples described in them and Mexico's Native Americans. He could see that many pre-Christian religions appeared to have some ideas in common—and discovered that some of those ideas were still to be found in the countryside of his own England. He began to collect and sort the bits of ethnography that had been appearing in travelers' accounts for centuries. Sorting meant that he had to find arrangements that allowed him first to keep track of them, and then to compare them.

In that process of organizing, Tylor made one of the most telling discoveries in the history of anthropology: he was the first to bring the idea of culture into a meaningful relation to the ethnographic facts that were piling up. The idea of culture was not exactly new; it had been bounced around among poets like Matthew Arnold and some of his German contemporaries. What Tylor *did* with it was unprecedented: he used the idea of culture to *explain* the facts that travelers had recorded among exotic peoples. Suddenly those facts were no longer mere curiosities—they made sense.

Cultural anthropology, as a discipline, had been born.

Tylor opens his 1871 book, *Primitive Culture*, with this passage:

> Culture or civilisation, taken in its wide ethnographic sense, is that complex whole which includes knowledge, belief, art, morals, law, custom and any other capabilities and habits acquired by man as a member of society.

Although history, geography, and religion had long offered more or less reasonable explanations for the differences among peoples, Tylor's cross-cultural approach proved far more useful and heuristic. It is difficult now to comprehend the views of human variation that preceded his, because we take the idea of culture and many of its implications for granted. But it wasn't always so. Columbus, for example, wondered whether the Amerindians whom he first encountered were actually human: they were so (culturally) different that he wasn't sure. This was an important question for Columbus—if these beings were human, they had to be converted; if they were not, they could be slaughtered like any other animal. It was an even more momentous question for Queen Isabella—the Pope told her that if these people were human, every murder of one of them would be a burden on her soul on Judgment Day. As it turns out, the Indians Columbus worried about soon became extinct at the hands of diseases introduced by his men; we don't know how much *that* cost Queen Isabella.

Before Tylor, differences among people had sometimes been accredited to separate thoughts of God. There is a large literature explaining (erroneously, of course) that climate caused what are now known to be cultural differences. For example: "hot" blood was said to be created by tropical climates, and that was the reason marriage practices there were different from those of Europe. Concern with race began to emerge in the late 1700s. Racial differences had been noted from time immemorial—there are portraits of Africans on ancient Greek vases. But assuming that racial differences affect the personal capacity for civilization was a wrong-headed idea that turned up only in the early 1800s and has been very hard to get rid of.

Tylor's own interest turned thus to comparison of the ethnographic facts found in different parts of the world. His *Primitive Culture* drew on ideas about evolution that were in the air at the time. As citizens of their time and culture, he and his cohorts made what we today consider some mistakes. One of the most egregious was to assume that present-day "primitive" people (to use their ethnocentric term) had got stuck in an earlier evolutionary stage of development, and were therefore just like the ancestors of people like Tylor himself. Following philosopher Herbert Spencer and some others, they arranged the differences in a line that seemed to them to run from simple to complex, and then turned the idea into a time line. It took a lot of decades to realize that non-Western people have as long a history as anybody else.

Something similar was going on in North America. Lewis Henry Morgan (1818–1881) was an American lawyer who grew up in New York State. Having become fascinated with the local Indians when he was a boy, he wrote *League of the Iroquois* (1851), still one of the best books about these people. In the process, Morgan learned that the Iroquoian terms for kinfolk did not classify relatives in the same way that English or Latin terms did. For example, in English the terms for Father's siblings' children and Mother's siblings' offspring are all the same: cousin. In Iroquois, however, although the relationship terms for Father's Brother's Son and Daughter are the same as for Mother's Sister's children, they are also identical to the terms for your own brother and sister. Moreover, a different set of terms indicates Father's Sister's and Mother's Brother's offspring. He realized that this implied that "family" meant different things in Iroquoian and Western societies.

When Morgan became an attorney for the New York Central Railroad, he went to the Middle West as part of his work. He talked with the Indians he found there. To his astonishment he found that although their language was completely different from Iroquois, they named their kinfolk in the same non-Western way that the Iroquoians did.

Morgan understood the importance of that discovery. He began to collect kinship terminologies from all over the world. He found that there were various ways to cut up the field of kinship as you name kinfolk. He ultimately found five of them. In the manner of the age, he gave them names derived from Greek words.

In order to make his work more comprehensive, Morgan got other people—travelers and missionaries—to collect kinship terms in many languages. He convinced the U.S. State Department in Washington to distribute his questionnaires to U.S. citizens living in many different parts of the world. Soon the data rolled in. Morgan organized it into a huge book, *Systems of Consanguinity and Affinity* (1871), which triggered anthropology's enduring fascination with kinship terminologies as keys to the social organization of small-scale societies.

Incidentally, kinship terms usually evolve very slowly. We in the United States today badly need terms to indicate the new sort of relationships that come with remarriage and other kinship aspects of modern life. We need new nomenclature to replace loaded terms like "stepmother," which has had bad press since the 1700s. What should you, a daughter of your father's first marriage, call the boy who shares your household who is a son from the first marriage of your father's second wife? What do you call the parents of your daughter's permanent live-in lover? Or the man who married your former wife?

Morgan made more or less the same mistakes that Tylor made—he assumed that one of these forms of kinship terminology was older than the others and that as cultural evolution occurred, they would change. He was wrong about that, but he made some major discoveries. Among the most important was the fact that people can logically divide up members of their families in different ways.

English-speakers have one term for their mothers and another (aunt) for her sisters. Iroquois call mother and her sisters all by the same term. This does *not* mean that the Iroquois don't know who their mother is (as was actually suggested early on); but that their mother and her sisters have some quality in common which it is necessary to emphasize. That quality turns out to be their shared membership in a clan. Iroquois are matrilineal, which means that eligibility for membership in a clan is determined by descent through female links only. In such a kinship system, your mother and her sisters all belong to the same clan: yours. If you are female, your children will, like you, belong to that same clan; if you are male, your children will belong to your wife's clan. Clans are normally exogamous, which means that marriage partners must be chosen from outside of it. Your father and his sisters and brothers necessarily belong to a different clan than your mother and you—otherwise your parents' marriage would have been considered incestuous. So the aunt on your father's side is not "family" in the same sense that the aunt on your mother's side is—and terminology indicates that crucial fact. Indeed, many people in the world do not have a word for what English-speakers today call a "family." But then, English lacks words for the specific familial focuses of other kinship systems; the best we can do is call them a "clan" (a Gaelic term still used in Scotland) or a "sept" (which means "division") or some other such word.

Although there are some errors in Morgan's lists, and although anthropology is now far beyond studying kinship terms out of the context of the rest of the culture, nevertheless those lists are still the most nearly complete ones we have.

At any rate, the invention of the culture concept gave people an objectively verifiable idiom in which to explain differences among peoples. That makes "culture" as momentous an idea as "species" is in biology. The term culture has now escaped into the general language: saying that people have a "different culture" is understood by everybody. It just means that they have an excuse for not being like you. But some usages are more sophisticated: most large corporations now realize that their establishment has a "corporate culture," and that some parts of it may not be shared by outsiders. Today, everybody "sort of knows" what culture is, and that general knowledge, we are convinced, has dulled our realization of the word's role in thinking about human differences. It is difficult now to remember what immense ignorances were suddenly banished when we acquired a word for what it is that makes aliens so different from us and from one another!

The cultural dimension is as diagnostic of human existence as the idea of "behavior" is to the study of all of animal life—including our own. It is as basic a breakthrough in thinking as the idea of "reaction" in chemistry; as fundamental as the idea of "axiom" in geometry; as important, indeed, as the idea of "zero" in mathematics.

Culture is, however, harder to pin down than any of those other insights. One reason is that your own culture always seems to be part of the "real world." We learn food preferences and prejudices as we learn to eat—and in many cases don't even know we have them until we are offered something and find that either its taste is repulsive or the *idea* of eating it is repulsive. We learn the names of birds and animals and flowers as we see them—and cannot imagine that other peoples see them differently just because they have different words for them. While most Europeans and North Americans are taught to identify plants by their flowers, many Africans can't tell one flower from another, but can readily identify plants by their leaves.

Culture differentiates people. Sometimes it differentiates us so much that we forget that we are all members of the same species—we let it turn us into battling partisans, forgetting our common humanity. Culture, in other words, not only makes us what we are—it can kill us.

Part II

Improving the Observers

The earliest efforts to improve the quality of our information about alien peoples were first to increase the number of observers and second to detect "false" information.

Chapter Five

The Beginnings of Ethnographic Fieldwork

Early anthropologists did not realize the importance of the context in which an ethnographic fact is found. They tried to collect information in a way they hoped would make the record "complete." Today we understand that context is an essential dimension and that no ethnographic record can ever be complete.

After the discovery of the idea of culture and the realization that one could ask people how they did things, the next major breakthrough was to teach the askers what the questions were. It was still assumed that a single set of questions would do for all cultures.

It often amazes people how long it took humanity to discover or accept ideas which to us, today, are self-evident. One thing this demonstrates, far better than changes in technology can, is that culture channels and determines human thought and perception. Until the 1800s, for example, everybody "knew" that men had more teeth than women. Ancient Greek philosophers had logically deduced that "fact," and what arrogance would induce one to argue with those Authorities-Of-Reference-for-all-Western-Thought? So until the advent of science, nobody thought to check mouths and count teeth. And when it came to the customs and motives of people in faraway places with strange-sounding names, conventional wisdom—a misnomer if ever there was one—clung tenaciously to the idea that you could treat them as if they were different animals, as was the custom in medieval "bestiaries." It is easy to laugh now, but even today you can still encounter the odd individual who professes absolute certainty that men must have fewer ribs than women. Because of Adam—that earliest ancestor who traded his rib for a wife in the book of Genesis—many people, it seems, would rather believe than know.

But not scientists. The idea that you can go and ask about custom and culture took shape in England and the United States at about the same time—

and, with a somewhat different philosophical base, also in Germany—but started from rather different assumptions in these countries.

In Britain the process began in what were called Discoverers' Clubs. The first "real" effort was to send an expedition to the Torres Strait Islands, which lie between Papua New Guinea and the Cape York Peninsula of Australia. That expedition (which included medical doctors, psychologists, and anthropologists who taught primarily about human origins) set out to study what they called "native" societies. They wanted to collect the "facts" themselves, in the belief that they themselves would get it "right," and they would never have to trust travelers again.

These researchers all had independent incomes, so expense was not a major consideration. A lot of information about Pacific Islanders, Australian aborigines, and tribal peoples of India was collected during this period.

During that same period, the British were developing a book of questions that they called *Notes and Queries in Anthropology*, whose last edition was published in the late 1940s. The book had questions and blank spaces where you could fill in the answers. You could, it was said, take it anywhere you went, ask the questions, fill in the blanks, and make a contribution to ethnography.

Actually, little worthwhile information was ever gathered on the basis of *Notes and Queries*. The reason is simple: a major part of training people to collect ethnographies lies in teaching them to discern whether a question is in fact understood by the person being questioned. You need to know enough about your informant (the person you are asking) to be able to tell whether he or she thinks it a sensible question. Only then can you begin to see how the answers fit together. *Notes and Queries in Anthropology* essentially denied any need for understanding what you heard: just fill in the blanks; after all, "those people" all have the same mental framework for their ideas and words.

Today we know that there can never be a complete "list of cultural elements" whose blanks you just fill in. In the first place, all of the people's own perception of their culture is lost in such a method. Translation problems are not even considered. Unless you understand the ideas and are very careful about how they are translated into English (or French, or whatever), the result is not merely lifeless but useless. Then too, every ethnographer must go beyond questioning into careful observation and description, because even when the question is perfectly understood and honestly answered, that answer may contradict actual behavior.

In the United States some of the same mistakes were made, as well as other, home-grown ones. The Bureau of American Ethnology (BAE) was organized in association with the Indian Service (then in the Department of War, later moved to the Department of the Interior) and with the Smithsonian Institution. The people who worked at the BAE were interested in what the Native Americans *had been* like before destructive waves of White immigrants descended on them. This was in the days before the dynamics of culture and its constantly changing nature were understood—a point we will examine later.

The American ethnographic tradition actually derives from Germany rather than England. Its founder, Franz Boas (1858–1942), had earned his doctorate at the University of Kiel in 1881. In 1883 he began a year-long scientific expedition to Baffin Island. There, intrigued with the Eskimos, he began to study their language, writing it down as they spoke. He even trained some of them to dictate it to him. This experience converted him to the study of anthropology. The main body of his ethnographic work was on the Kwakiutl of Vancouver Island in British Columbia.

Franz Boas became the undisputed father of cultural anthropology in the United States. He championed the idea of "texts" as devices by which one could simultaneously study language and culture, and advocated "total recovery" of ethnographic data before any generalization was attempted. Unlike the so-called "unilinear evolutionists" who focused on the similarities among cultures, Boas stressed cultural differences and ascribed them to the diverging and ultimately unique historical development of evolving societies.

During his many years at Columbia University he trained almost all the important North American anthropologists in the first half of the twentieth century, imbuing them with his own holistic approach to fieldwork and a sense that the discipline was grounded in the four fields of archaeological, cultural, linguistic, and physical anthropology. The Boasian school enshrined *culture* as the key concept in North American anthropology and brought us two ideas which are debated to this day: *cultural relativism* and *cultural determinism*.

Boas established the *International Journal of American Linguistics*, and was a founder of the American Anthropological Association. He made it a tenet of the anthropological worldview that all human races have an equal capacity to develop culture, and that all behavioral differences among populations result from cultural, not racial or genetic, causes.

In establishing culture as the key concept of anthropology, and stressing that the uniqueness of each culture results from its specific and singular historical development, Boasian thought marks North American anthropology to this day. We owe Boas something else: anthropological societies had admitted women since the nineteenth century; Matilda Cox Stevenson studied Native Americans in the southwestern United States and in Mexico before Boas got to Columbia. But Boas actively *encouraged* women (including Ruth Benedict and Margaret Mead) to enter the field. In the 1980s, anthropology became the first traditional discipline to award more doctoral degrees to women than to men.

Chapter Six

Participant Observation

"Participant observation" means that the ethnographer participates in the life of the people in order to discover what the right questions are. Two factors limit participant observation: what those people will put up with and what the personality of the fieldworker will allow. Only if ethnographers learn to speak with people in their own language can they understand the rational reasons people have for doing what they do.

One international incident during the First World War made an immense impact on the development of ethnography. A Polish anthropologist named Bronislaw Malinowski, who had studied in London, found himself in the Trobriand Islands near the eastern tip of New Guinea, which were at that time a British dependency. With the declaration of war, Malinowski became technically an enemy alien because his citizenship was Polish and the Poles were "on the other side." The British and Australians were reasonable, however: they told Malinowski that if he would stay in the Trobriand Islands, they would not imprison him (as they would be forced to do if he returned to Britain or to Australia).

Malinowski settled in. He perfected his use of the Trobriand language—not just as an object of study, but as "the way to talk." He saw few outsiders; Trobrianders became his primary companions. He got to know them well—not as sources for texts, but as people to talk to when he was lonely.

When Malinowski returned to England after the war, he examined his experiences closely and described a form of field research that we today call participant observation. That is to say: the ethnographer lives with the people he or she studies, as closely as they will allow, and as fully as he or she can tolerate.

Malinowski did not exactly invent participant observation—Americans like Frank Cushing did it years earlier among the Zuni, but never recognized that it was a method of research. However, Malinowski *did* formalize the method as a basis for writing ethnography, and he *did* train a whole generation of anthropologists to do ethnography that way. Today every adequate ethnographer does his or her fieldwork in the native tongue of the people being studied.

Malinowski thus transposed the importance of language into a new key. Whereas Boas had been meticulous about collecting texts that were dictated by the people being studied, in their language, Malinowski wandered around among the people, talking to them—in their language—about what they were doing. The difference was considerable. For several decades, it had a large effect on the different ways in which ethnography was pursued by the British (following Malinowski) and by the Americans (following Boas).

Malinowski's interest focused on improving understanding of the cultural customs. He found that the best way to do that was to get the language right. He took some of his field notes in the Trobriand language. Excerpts sometimes showed up in his published writings. But his fieldwork goals did not include any study of linguistics. He insisted that in order to follow what was going on, a fieldworker had to learn to talk the way the informants talked.

It is important to realize that if you learn to speak a language well, you can dispense with an interpreter. Using an interpreter means that the most fundamental analysis of the culture is done by that person—not by the ethnographer. Interpreters necessarily bias information because, even though they may know both languages well, their major effort is putting what the informant is saying into terms the anthropologist already knows. This blocks the opportunity for the ethnographer to examine his or her own culture as well as the intricacies and uniquenesses of the informants' language as new ideas emerge—indeed, an ethnographer with a good interpreter may not even recognize that there are new ideas to be dealt with.

Malinowski was not "against" linguistics. However, the anthropology he learned and practiced did not include anything about linguistics as a science. The loss to linguistic anthropology was considerable. But Malinowski was left free to think about the importance of ethnography as an element in the science of anthropology. By not considering "the text" a useful product in itself, he showed us how to use texts in the interest of ethnography rather than in the interest of linguistics.

Malinowski's ethnography of the Trobriand Islands was reported in a series of specialized monographs—one on economy and trade (*Argonauts of the Western Pacific*), one on kinship, family and sexuality (*The Sexual Life of Savages*), one on farming and gardening (*Coral Gardens and their Magic*). There were others on law and on economy.

As the result of all this documentation, his work on the Trobriand Islanders set a standard to which all other ethnographies aspired. The Trobrianders joined the Kwakiutl in occupying special positions of honor in the history of ethnography.

A few ethnographers have restudied the Trobriand Islands. The most important work was done by Annette Weiner some fifty years after Malinowski was there. She still found much of what Malinowski had reported. She also added important details—about the position of women in trade, for example—

which Malinowski had not mentioned at all and which not only filled out the record but illuminated some parts of Malinowski's work that had been unclear.

In the process, Weiner showed yet again that ethnographers ignore women (or anybody else) only at their peril. "Getting it complete" had come to mean that you have to talk to everybody about everything. And that, obviously, isn't possible. Thus we are also reminded that no ethnography is ever complete.

Even the simplest of cultures is vastly more complex than the mind of any single person, whether native or observer, can encompass. The ethnographer sees as much as there is time for, and explains as much as possible in the terms of the people who live the lives they are reporting. It is an honorable and demanding goal—and one that can never be reached.

The practice of participant observation made one factor clear: any ethnographer, in learning new ways of looking at the world, risks immense emotional distress. Ethnographers have to tolerate and learn from this reaction: psychological dislocation is part of the learning process. Fieldwork is aimed at understanding—at best, what the people mean by what they do, but in any case understanding something beyond what you already know. Without undergoing culture shock, you cannot work through the cultural dissonances within you that prevent those comprehensions.

Knowingly subjecting yourself to culture shock is very daunting, however, and the subsequent history of ethnography is full of people who used methodology, the mechanical process of gathering data, to defend themselves against such anxieties. Imitating experimental psychologists in a laboratory, some fieldworkers distance themselves emotionally from the people they are trying to understand—as in, "We parachuted in for a day or two and came out with the specific information we needed." Most such attempts at preventing culture shock, even when dignified with titles like "experimental" fieldwork, are no better than tourism, because the researchers came out as they went in: with all their prejudices intact. When you examine such work closely, you almost always find that its preoccupation with method is a defense at not measuring up as a participant observer.

We'll return to this topic in chapter 14. But for now: Any promise that you can encounter the Other without being forced to question your own assumptions or being burdened by culture shock is a guarantee that you will learn little of substance.

Chapter Seven

Using Alien Ideas to
Examine Our Own

Examining our own culture in terms of some Others' is the best way yet found to make us aware of the shortcomings, quirks, and victories of our culture and to grasp the assumptions we don't always know we make.

We have already noted—and will note again as the book proceeds—that you cannot learn another culture without taking a deeper look at your own. That deeper look can be turned into ethnographic analysis almost as readily as the look you gave your subject culture—in other words, you can learn to be objective about your own way of life. Ethnography thus offers you a domain for studying two cultures, using each to expose ideas in the other. Most fieldworkers turn away from facts about their own culture to concentrate on the alien one. But you *can* do both.

Margaret Mead did her major fieldwork on the South Pacific islands of Samoa and Bali, and among several groups in New Guinea. She published accounts of her work in monographs of the American Museum of Natural History, but she also wrote books that used her work in those societies to illuminate the culture of the United States.

In 1928, she published *Coming of Age in Samoa*. Its express purpose was to show that North Americans and Europeans made a very heavy trip of adolescence (and seventy years later she is probably still right about it being hell to be fifteen years old in Europe and the United States, for all that it is a different kind of hell than it was when she wrote). But she went on to say that we were wrong when we blamed the stresses of teen-age life on the physiology of growth and maturation. Mead's rather daring point was that adolescent problems originate in culture, and are not an unavoidable by-product of the hormonal changes unleashed when young people reach sexual maturity. There is still a lot of argument about whether she was right.

A few years later, in 1935, she published *Sex and Temperament in Three Primitive Societies*, which was about gender and the division of labor into women's work and men's work. Her point in this book was that the sexual division of labor in the Western World was (except for the facts of reproduction) *not* due to our biology but, again, a cultural product. She described three New Guinea peoples, each of whom divided up gender responsibilities differently from one another, and who all did it differently from the usual Western way.

She had now put before her own people the startling ideas that adolescence was turned into an ordeal by culture and that gender roles are culturally, not biologically, determined.

People do not like having their basic premises challenged, and academics are no different. Mead was roundly criticized by some of her colleagues for using alien data to illuminate North American culture. Some even claimed that she made up her facts. She didn't. Some accused her of sloppy and biased fieldwork. It wasn't. A few said that what she did wasn't anthropology. It was, and it made anthropology reflexive and thereby relevant in a way it never was before. The immense popularity of Mead's work greatly stimulated the political effort to equalize educational and employment opportunities for the sexes. So if you are female and pursuing a career in any field which was once an exclusively male prerogative, hoist a glass to Margaret Mead.

Mead had another impact on her own culture that is less often noticed. When her daughter, Mary Catherine Bateson, was a baby, her pediatrician was a doctor named Benjamin Spock. Mead was far too canny and curious to leave the child-rearing propensities of her own society unexamined. She was not *about* to do something just because it was the custom. She also knew a lot about how babies were tended in New Guinea and in Bali. Dr. Spock listened well. The result is that Margaret Mead's footprints are all over Dr. Spock's *The Common Sense Book of Baby and Child Care*, which has sold more copies than any other original title ever published in English, and millions more in foreign languages. Spock's book completely altered people's thinking about babies and how we should rear them. Who says that ethnographers don't have an impact? Don't sneer just because, thirty years later, people say they think Spock was wrong. Culture has indeed changed, but every one of us who grew up in the Spock period or the post-Spock period has had a much easier and pleasanter childhood than we would have had without him—or without Margaret Mead.

In the late 1970s, when Mead was safely silenced by death, Derek Freeman (a New Zealander who had done fieldwork in Samoa some years after Mead) wrote a book once again declaring Mead's material to be not only "wrong" but a total misrepresentation of the "real" Samoa. He "deduced" that she had twisted her data and even accused her of having made them up to support her points about North Americans.

The resulting "Freeman brouhaha" within the tight little world of professional anthropology forced the discipline's practitioners to face once again two important questions—and do it with more care: (1) how do you judge the accuracy of ethnographic data? and (2) how do you deal with apparent contradictions in the data supplied at different times by different anthropologists?

Note that these are variants of the same question, because each can be treated as a subset of the other.

Assuming that one investigator must be "right" and the other therefore "wrong" had reduced the problem to hopelessly simplistic terms and prevented its solution. When two ethnographers report on the same trait or event, each may have been looking at different aspects of what was being observed, and almost certainly each began from different premises. That perspective makes differences unavoidable, and the problem of reliability insoluble.

The dilemma is similar to that which juries face when different eyewitnesses offer quite different evidence. To judge the trustworthiness of ethnographic observations we, like juries, need to know what each "witness" was doing—and why each saw the same situation differently.

The question therefore became: is there such a thing as "correct" ethnographic data in the sense that we can have "correct" data in the natural sciences? If you, an anthropologist, are going to use somebody else's ethnographic data, what standards do you use to evaluate their reliability?

It soon became clear that the ethnographer has to help the reader by expressing as clearly as possible what premises and assumptions guided the work. We are forced to realize that facts in ethnography are far more complex than facts in physical sciences such as chemistry. Neither chemical nor ethnographic facts can be separated from the observer, but laboratory experiments allow a chemist to minimize context by controlling every variable except the ones chosen for observation. For ethnographers, however, part of the task is to determine what is context and what is subject, and how subject and context influence each other. Precisely because context is *always* part of ethnographic observation, it can never be totally controlled for; ethnographers consequently have far more trouble agreeing on what they see than chemists do, and replicability—a *sine qua non* of natural science—can only be approximated, never achieved. You really cannot step into the same river of evolving culture twice. Chemists would never put up with such ambiguity, but for the study of culture, a tolerance for ambiguity is a primary prerequisite.

This ambiguity means, however, that you can probably support any claim you like by quoting *somebody's* statement that "the Bongo-bongo do it that way"—which is to admit that ethnography (like everything else) can be used for evil purposes as well as for good. Missionaries have been known to use phony ethnography to increase contributions to their missions. Businesspeople and developers have been known to use an ethnographer's hard-won insight into some society's religion or social organization to cheat its people out of their territory or resources.

At this point, the problem of ethnographic reliability sprouted new questions: are anthropologists responsible for figuring out their own culture? Where does anthropology stop and other uses of ethnography begin? And most important of all: what is the ethnographer's responsibility for the misuse of her or his intellectual product?

A few years after Margaret Mead, that issue came to be a central concern for anthropological ethnographers.

Chapter Eight

Comparing Cultures

Comparison among many different cultures has taught us at least two things: (1) all human populations face the same common problems, but each addresses them in a different way, and (2) all the parts of any culture are interrelated.

When Tylor defined culture, he meant the term to denote innate human capacity for *learning* any lifeway. Any normal baby can learn to speak any language and will just as readily absorb the habits of thought and action and evaluation of the people who care for her. There is no biological reason whatsoever why you should resemble your parents in your work, your values, or your lifestyle. This makes our species the most adaptive of all life forms because we can adapt culturally as well as biologically. But it also makes us totally dependent on culture.

The recognition that culture is always acquired "locally"—the source of its variability—soon led to a quite different but equally important use of the term "culture": it became the label for any specific population's traditional lifeway. Ethnographers spoke of Arapaho culture; of Balinese culture; of Chinese, Dahomean, and Eskimo culture. There really should have been two terms: one for humanity's characteristic mode of acquiring and inventing behavior, the other to identify a specific society's characteristic customs and rituals, its technologies, organizations, values, and language.

But there aren't. And we still haven't invented a fool-proof, noncontroversial method for determining where one culture ends and another begins.

Many bits and pieces of culture are shared by many different peoples. That fact is not as important as this one: whatever particular bunch of cultural ideas you examine, they are fitted together with other idea-bundles in something unique and distinctive. The way traits are fitted together creates the character of a culture—*not* the mere presence of the traits themselves. To approach this from another perspective: the *meaning* of what appear superfi-

cially to be identical facts in different systems is a function of their local interaction with other facts.

Organization and context thus underlie all comparison of ideas. The way
context works seems to us to be one of the basic questions of social science.

Comparison, however, if done sensitively, can begin the process of solving
this problem. Comparison is a systematic examination of traits (as originally
understood in the context of the cultures where they originated) in a specially
manufactured context called "science" (for lack of a better word). In this new
context, the idea does not depend for its validity on any of the cultural assumptions which produced it. All we have to do is figure out how, when we lift a
"datum" out of context, it can be made to bring some part of the context with
it.

The notion of systematically comparing one culture with another is at
least as old as Tylor. He was, in the last decades of the nineteenth century, the
first to count the number of different cultures that exhibited what seemed to
him to be "the same" trait, then attempt a statistical analysis of how many cultures did and how many did not exhibit it. In Tylor's day, we must remember,
statistics was still a seriously underdeveloped field. But we also have to remember that such a method of comparison risks stripping cultural elements out of
the context that gives them meaning. You have to be *very* careful to insure that
the new context into which you put them is the realm of theory and *not* the
realm of fiction.

Boas responded to Tylor's argument by emphasizing the importance of
the very context that Tylor's way of thinking ignored. That problem about context has never been settled: there are still people who examine and compare
culture traits outside of the context that gives them meaning. The issue continues to bedevil all comparison.

There are other problems. Say you are counting a trait such as polygyny
among the Great Plains tribes, and you come to the Blackfoot Indians of the
1800s. The Blackfoot Federation included the Piegan, the Blood, and the
Northern Blackfoot who all lived virtually identical lifeways in contiguous territories. Do you judge them to be a single culture, or do you count them as
three? Your decision, either way, could seriously skew your statistics. Anthropologists were a long time learning that using "a culture" as the unit for statistical comparison engenders difficulties that may make anything you can
learn that way marginal. And yet, in many contexts there simply is no way to
avoid talking about "a" culture.

In the process, anthropologists realized at the theoretical level something that fieldworkers had long known: the various parts of a culture really
do hang together. Only if contradictory bits of a culture never appear in the
same context can they remain contradictory—the inconsistencies never show
up. When people actually see a disparity between cultural bits in the same context, they work to eliminate it. But if disparities appear only in separate contexts, they can stay unrecognized and be ignored.

Thus, again, it is the way the cultural bits provide each other's context
that makes the telling difference. If you separate a single trait out for compar-

ison, you lose the self-correcting mechanism provided by context. The "same" trait may mean quite different things, depending on time and place, participants, and observers. If you fail to account for that difference, you'll be unwittingly comparing apples and oranges.

Ruth Benedict, a brilliant and intuitive anthropologist at Columbia University (she also published poetry) did not exactly solve this problem, but she *did* find a way to get around it. Benedict knew perfectly well that her own middle-class North American culture contained too many unanalyzed assumptions and biases to make a suitable yardstick for other cultures. She began the search for what we might call the "spirit" or essence of several cultures—a primitive way of setting the idea of context to one side (or, if you prefer, of summing it up in one word). She then compared such "spirits." The way she did it was to start not from the ethnography itself, but from distinctions made by Western philosophers. In emphasizing the differences in "spirit" among the cultures she examined, she could ignore not only the many similarities in their traits, but the organization of traits within each.

In her first important book, *Patterns of Culture* (1934), Benedict elaborated a distinction first made by the German poet and philosopher Nietzsche. She contrasted Dyonisian behavior (loud and emotional) and Apollonian behavior (in quiet good taste and intellectual). Her next step was to classify Boas's Kwakiutl of the North Pacific Coast as Dionysian, and the Zuni of the American Southwest desert as Apollonian. (Benedict had visited the Zuni, but she was not a successful fieldworker—she herself asserted that the reason was that she was deaf. Her capacity to read lips in English, however, was astonishing; I have watched her do it across a wide and noisy room.) Benedict then added a third group: the Dobuans who live on a small island near New Guinea, who had been studied by Reo Fortune. To describe the Dobuans, Benedict went to psychiatry rather than philosophy—she called them "schizophrenic."

Benedict was among to first to posit that if you had been raised a Zuni, that fact alone would make you different from what you would have been if your identical-DNA body had been raised a Dobuan or a Kwakiutl. That *statement* is correct, but it would be several decades before our knowledge of the relationship between culture and personality would allow us to understand it thoroughly. Benedict's approach to explaining the *process*—in terms of the "spirit" of a culture—was not exactly wrong, but it very soon proved to be inadequate. You simply cannot sum up a culture in a single concept not native to it, and then compare it with others that have been depicted in different monistic terms. But no one could know that until she tried.

Patterns of Culture was widely read and became one of the most influential books ever published by an anthropologist. Ruth Benedict's legacy is our awareness that people of different cultures interpret life differently. That insight added significantly to our realization that *if you judge one culture by the standards of another, you will misrepresent both.*

Chapter Nine

The Morass of
Cultural Relativism

Cultural relativism is a doctrine that insists that any human action is to be judged by the ideas and purposes of the actors, not those of the spectator. There is no way to say that one culture is "better" than another until you can answer the question, "Better at doing what?"

As people of good will and discernment, Franz Boas and Bronislaw Malinowski were dedicated to the proposition that in order to understand the ethnography of another culture, you have to know what the people who live it are trying to do with it. Boas fought long and hard against the very human tendency of judging foreigners and their alien lifeways in terms of the ideas of your own culture—especially if you did it without ever noticing that they had ideas that they used as assumptions or premises, the way geometry uses axioms.

Boas insisted on what he called "cultural relativism" (not cultural *relativity*, which it is sometimes mistakenly called). He meant that every culture is to be judged by its own premises. And *that* means by its own axioms—the assumptions which people themselves make about their society, their environment, their technology and religion and science.

The opposite of cultural relativism is some form of "ethnocentrism." Ethnocentrism means that you call upon only your own premises, the axioms of your own culture, when you judge others. But because cultural relativism is much more complex than that, ethnocentrism is no *mere* "opposite." Ethnocentrism means that you do not give foreigners credit for knowing much of anything—they haven't done it your way, so they can't be very smart.

Both cultural relativism and ethnocentrism are such simple responses that they are sometimes a little hard to accept. What makes them difficult is that they require you to realize that you yourself operate from a bunch of assumptions and premises that determine your own view of the world. That

33

idea isn't difficult to grasp, but believing it enough actually to apply to yourself may be. You may find it all but impossible to determine when you are doing it.

Some people, not realizing that they are being ethnocentric, and not comprehending the implications of cultural relativism, believe that cultural relativism means that "one culture is as good as another." That, of course, is not only incorrect, it is errant nonsense. It could be not-wrong only if you can be very sure that you are using an objective yardstick for judging how one culture is better. If your standard is an ethnocentric one, be careful—you may be missing something. You may even be blindly narrow-minded.

What the principle of cultural relativism *does* say is that when you judge another culture, you do so on the basis of certain premises. Those may very well not be the correct ones from the standpoint of the people living the culture. Likely you are judging on the basis of your own culture's assumptions, unthinkingly assuming that they are universal. For the truly ethnocentric, premises are always the same everywhere, as they are in mathematics—but don't forget that people like the ancient Near Easterners counted in base-6, or that some Africans count in base-20 instead of in base-10 as the industrialized world does. Don't forget that the Japanese pointed off numbers in units of four instead of units of three until they changed that after World War II. And to this day, when nearly all other nations have embraced the decimal system (how base-10 can you get?), the United States persists in a measuring system with 12 inches to the foot, 36 inches to the yard, and 5,280 feet to the mile.

The point is this: if you claim that one culture is as good as another, you have to ask "good at what?" By whose definitions and prejudices?

It is, of course, possible to discover ways of comparing cultures that examine their relative efficiency in doing what everybody agrees has to be done. Leslie A. White, for example, developed a schema for comparing the energy efficiency of societies in using their resources, and concluded that those who are more efficient tend to supplant those who are less so.

It is popular in our own culture today to rank other societies on the basis of what we North Americans call "human rights," but you should remember that such philosophical concepts, no matter how benign their intent, do not describe universals. You can also compare cultures on the way they use ideas like beauty, but again, if you do, remember that standards of beauty change from one place and historical era to another. Or how about "Progress," that modern shibboleth? If society X attacks malaria-carrying mosquitoes with DDT and manages to cut its death rate from the disease by 50 percent, does that prove society X's culture is superior to that of its neighbor, society Y, which has not done so? How about in the long run, when X has a population explosion (because so few people die of malaria now) which leads to twice as many deaths from starvation as it used to have from malaria, while Y continues as it always has? Is Progress *really* our most important product? Is it even definable?

Cultural relativism as policy usually does not work. The reason is that most people, the world across, are not willing to intellectualize their own values to the point that they can concede to Others the right to have different ones. Consider cannibalism: nobody thinks it is "better" than noncannibalism—not even cannibals. However, cannibals may have ideas about eating human flesh that are so complex, so indispensable to the way they view everything else, and so logical, that they are reluctant to give them (and it) up—not because they like eating people (they may find the meat tasty, but that is another issue), but because they do not know any other way to achieve what they tell themselves eating human flesh allows them to achieve. This is a difficult moral point. What do you do with dedicated cannibals?

Colonial powers were all immensely ethnocentric—they destroyed cultures knowingly because otherwise they could not impose their own ways and their own ideas on the people they wanted to rule and tax and profit from. Colonials traditionally used missionaries as their frontline assault troops against local tradition and custom. Of course this did not always work out as expected: like the earliest anthropological ethnographers (who were also hired to aid colonial administrations), missionaries often became effective champions of the natives.

The major mission denominations, especially in Europe, taught and expected a lot more than mere "conversion of the savages." It is fair to say that their missionaries contributed greatly to the birth of ethnography, indeed of anthropological science, and that they did (and still do) what they set out to do, which was to reduce human suffering. We owe a lot to those of them for whom ethnography was both a source and a goal.

But it is also true that human beings can convince themselves more easily of something if they can convince others first. That is, after all, how salespeople are trained. Especially in the United States, the more openly anti-intellectual sects have habitually sent out missionaries who conspicuously lack the training and temperament for working with Others. Ignorant of the lifeways of those they are to "serve," and armed only with the ability to quote Scripture on any subject, these hopeless ethnocentrics espouse intolerant, ethnocentric dogmas. In many cases, the purpose in sending such misfits is obviously as much an attempt to "strengthen their faith in the crucible," that is, "to save the souls of the missionaries," as to improve the lives they touch in the field.

Note here that the urge to proselytize is not restricted to those imbued with a sacred spirit: there are equally committed "missionaries" for secular ideologies like communism, capitalism, and free market principles; their sins are as great—sometimes worse.

It is doubtful that most of the dedicated young fanatics who went out (and still go!) to remote societies to spread their gospels or their political economies had any idea of the harm they do to the people they meet. But they have helped destroy the bulk of good-enough cultures, and they have stolen life's meaning and the independence and personal dignity of millions of decent people.

And today? Who's ethnocentric? What ideas out there are to be destroyed? What ones are to be honored? Which are destined—like Islam and Christianity, Capitalism and Communism—to be imposed by fire and sword? We have arrived at the rock-bottom moral question. Should you, for reasons that you have been taught to believe necessary and sufficient, interfere in the lives of Others? What if they did that to you?

We may have come a long way since the first protohuman picked up a burning branch to begin domesticating fire, but our fundamental moral questions are just as slippery and difficult as they ever were.

Chapter Ten

Premises and Ethnography

One of the most important tasks of any ethnographer is to figure out the premises—the axioms or assumptions—on which people's reasoning is based. As we do that for strangers, our own (formerly unconscious) premises become illuminated.

The next stage is explaining the rationale—the logic—of the institutions that people live by. You cannot profitably ask people *why* they do things as they do. Their way is obvious and correct to them. They never have to think about "why"—that is a foreigner's question. Who, in our own culture, considers the rationale of "things we know how to do without reflecting on them?" Why do men's shirts button left-over-right and women's the other way? Why is the clutch to the left and the gas-pedal on the right? As a child, I was taught that the answer to all such questions is: "No matter how dark the night, I'm still your mother." I (still) guess that meant that questions about the obvious deserve a snide reply.

What you, the ethnographer, have to do is figure it out for yourself. However, you must also check your explanation with the people to be sure you have it right. But you should be aware that whereas, before you figured it out, *you* were in mental country you never considered before, now when you ask them to check your thinking, you put *them* into mental country they never before considered. If you are right, they will probably ask you what you think they have been trying to tell you all this time. If you are wrong, they will probably flatly tell you so. But sometimes they'll get so excited insisting that is *not* the way things are, that you may safely assume you've got it approximately right but that you have just blurted out a truth they've gone to great lengths to hide from themselves.

Finding the rationale for Others' behavior makes it obvious, if you do it right, that no people is "primitive" and that Others never do things simply because they "don't know any better."

37

You will find that their ways of doing things are usually as sensible as our own, *if* you start from the same premises or assumptions as they do. Human institutions are *never* foolish. Their ways, like some of our own, may be inefficient. But they are *not* stupid.

This brings up another important point: understanding and explaining the rationale behind what people do will suddenly bring ethnography and "theory" into a single camp. Boas, who operated according to Johann Gottfried Herder's (1744–1803) dictum that language is the very soul of any ethnic group, maintained that you should not worry about theory until you have enough facts for a firm basis for understanding—and by and large Boas never got very deeply into theory. Today much ethnography stems from the opposite idea: that understanding *why* people do it the *way* they do it *is* the theory.

Malinowski showed that the people he called "natives" were sensible folk. The next stage was to look into the way they explained to themselves what they did. Among the foremost proponents of this "new" kind of explanation was E. E. Evans-Pritchard.

In 1926 when he was twenty-four years old, Edward Evan Evans-Pritchard (whom everybody called E-P), went to do fieldwork in the Sudan. He was a student of Malinowski, but the two men seem to have been designed to dislike one another (actually, the word "dislike" here is typical British understatement). E-P went to the Sudan at the request and the expense of Charles Gabriel Seligmann, one of the medical doctors associated with the Torres Straits expedition. E-P handed his notes from that first trip—his original studies—to Seligmann. Seligmann and his wife Brenda then published them under their own names. When asked about that, E-P shrugged that the notes were Seligmann's property because he, E-P, had been paid to go get them.

But when Evans-Pritchard returned to the southern Sudan a few years later, he went as his own man. He conducted a long-term study of the Azande people. Years later he could still speak their language, and he spent the rest of his life writing articles about them. His major achievement from that field job was *Witchcraft, Oracles, and Magic among the Azande* (1937). This book shows why, given Azande premises, their witchcraft beliefs are perfectly sensible; if you are going to attack Azande beliefs, you will have to attack their premises, *not* their logic or rationality.

The most salient premise of Azande witchcraft beliefs (as in much of traditional Africa) is that all human misfortune, including disease, results from the ill will and actions of other human beings. Science can more or less prove this Azande premise to be inadequate—germs and viruses do exist; accidents do occur. Science can often provide more elegant explanations. But science can *not* "prove" folk premises to be false. Compared to science they can sometimes be seen as simplistic, mythical, or leading people into ineffectiveness and discomfort. But they can not be "proved" wrong. The difficulty is in the premises. There is an immense difference between proving that something is true and not being able to prove that it is not true—the latter allows you to hold on to inadequate premises.

E-P's point is that premises are not mere nonsense. Azande premises dictate that a belief in spirits and witches is sensible. Some of us do not believe that to be the case—but that is beside the point. The point is: if you began your reasoning where the Azande do, you would logically come to much the same conclusion as they do.

Evans-Pritchard thus demonstrated that Azande reason just as logically as any other people. He also pointed out (and this is even more important) that *we are all—every one of us—slaves to our premises*. Like the axioms in geometry, your premises are the basis from which you begin your reasoning—the assumptions you make as a foundation for reasoning. If you change your premised axioms (as those of Euclidean geometry are changed for non-Euclidean geometry) your reasoning will take you to very different conclusions.

Thus, *Witchcraft, Oracles and Magic* brought to the fore a proposition that has stayed there ever since: if you want to know why any people, including your own, do some of the things they do, you have to figure out what their premises, their unchallenged assumptions, are.

But that is like asking: what are the premises of our own science? our own religion? our own ideas about law? It is not surprising that people can almost never tell you what their premises are—people don't think about premises until they are either pushed hard or trained well. Still, if you figure them out correctly and ask if you are right, they may get quite patronizing and tell you that of course that's right, how could it be anything else?

This realization about premises lies at the heart of the study of any religion. One difficulty in writing about such supernatural tenets as witchcraft ideas arises out of the singularity that religion is the only major human activity without a biological foundation. Saying that is not to deny that the anxieties associated with death, illness, and misfortune may well be necessary and sufficient causes for the rise of supernatural beliefs. But religion is a cultural phenomenon. (If, in the future, such a biological "cause" is ever found, we may have to eat these words—but not yet.)

To fill that biological void, scholars and philosophers and theologians have created a huge literature about religion and the "proper" way to think about it. That literature is *not* based on actions the way most other ethnographic "facts" can be. People everywhere perform observable ceremonies; they have ideas about the "unknown" that they can explain to you. Their explanations are the only "facts" there are. Comparison of such facts from several societies is not grounded—*cannot* be grounded—in the same objective reality as a comparison of farming methods or household formation. Too many anthropologists, in writing about religion, have overlooked the fact that religion is *purely* ideas, with no basis in material reality. Let it be understood that we are *not* proffering a judgment on whether any specific religion is true or false. As with other ultimately untestable axioms or hypotheses, the value of any ideology can only be judged by those who actually live and think in accordance with its premises.

Evans-Pritchard also worked for a long time among the Nuer—a Sudanese people totally unrelated to, and totally unlike, the Azande. The Nuer came from a different language group and are herders of cattle, whereas the Azande are farmers. E-P wrote three specialized ethnographies about them: *The Nuer* (which is about the way they run their politics in the absence of a state mechanism), *Kinship and Marriage among the Nuer*, and *Nuer Religion*. Their aim was to examine not only the ethnography of what the people being studied do, but to compare their ideas about what they do with notions held by other peoples doing something similar. Last but not least, E-P aimed to test their fit with earlier explanations anthropologists and other social scientists had put forward. Thus, each book turned out to be not only ethnography, but theory.

The specialized ethnography, in this sense, has risen above being merely a device for recording the ways of some alien people. They have become a prototype for what anthropologists need to consider when they attempt comparisons. Since E-P's Nuer work, you can compare ethnographically derived premises instead of, like Benedict, trusting philosophers to do it for you.

Chapter Eleven

Their Culture—and Yours

It is pretty obvious that Others have a culture. It is more difficult to realize that you have one too. Your culture may be very strange by other people's standards. And it may keep you from understanding theirs.

When you go to the field as an ethnographer, you almost inadvertently learn as much about yourself and your own culture as about the people you are studying. The situations which throw new light on the familiar usually appear to be of minor importance while they are happening. But they add up. As you become more and more comfortable in *their* culture, your own culture begins to seem weird.

We're back to our old refrain again: in learning to be human, we master one (or at most three or four) of the uncountable ways to be a cultured being. If some lesson is not to be found in your environment, you cannot learn it. If it *is* there, you may avoid it but you cannot totally ignore it.

All this means, ironically enough, that learning any one way of being human makes all the other ways foreign—perhaps to the point of seeming repulsively alien. Yet if you examine alien customs closely, you will find that they are not really incomprehensible, just unfamiliar.

The first day I was in the field with the Tiv, an elder came to pay a call. He had heard me say (through an interpreter—the last time I used one) that I wanted to learn the Tiv language. To most people everywhere, language learning begins with acquiring a vocabulary. To him, the most important words to know were the names of people and plants. He brought three wives and several kids bearing armloads of plants. He told me the names of the wives and the kids. I learned them readily.

He then told the children to spread the plants out on the ground. There were about a dozen different varieties. He began drilling me in the names. I had great difficulty: not with the names but with distinguishing one plant from the next. Once I began to get them right, he had the kids mix them up—and I was back at square one: those plants all looked pretty much alike to me. My gut

41

reaction was that I was inadequately prepared for fieldwork because I had never taken a course in botany.

After that experience of proving to one and all what a poor student I was, I thought a lot about those plants. I had been taught, by my mother and my grandfather and a lot of other people, to identify plants by their flowers. The man who brought his wives and children became a friend—indeed, he helped more than he ever knew in my efforts to learn his language. One day, several months later, I brought him six flowers and asked him to identify them. He could not. But we both came to understand the point: he had learned to identify plants by their leaves, but I had learned to identify them by their flowers. We each learned something about ourselves by learning something about each other.

Two more examples will be enough: in the Tiv language, no one ever has to take the rap for anything. In English we say "I dropped it." In Tiv we say "it dropped [away from] me." In English, "I" did it. In Tiv, "it" did it—I was not at fault. English contains example after example of expressions that "blame" somebody for whatever happens. Tiv lacks the "blame." You are never inadequate or clumsy in Tiv because Tiv language "blames" the thing, not the person (we do the same thing when we say "*It* rains"). Of course you hear things like "The door hit me." A child may say "The milk spilled." In my culture, *it* seems to me (!), people feel a lot more guilt than Tiv are called upon to feel. (You are invited to disagree—especially if you have some evidence from some language in addition to English.)

And then there are the words for colors. In English, color words are, for the most part, adjectives: the *green* hat; the *red* sunset. In Tiv, colors are verbs. The hat *greens* (their word *ii* does not mean what green means in English because it includes blue). The sunset *reds*. The message—the basic idea—is simple in both languages. But the way it is communicated changes the idea ever so slightly. Both approaches are easy to understand and to use. But each reflects a different view of the world. All human languages so far reported have words at least for light-colored, dark-colored, and red. Beyond that, how you divide the spectrum into colors is a function of culture. If Tiv want to separate green from blue they use metaphors: plant colored or sky colored.

As we learn a new language, we come to realize that there is no "right" way to see or to say anything. But there *is* viewpoint. Viewpoints not only vary, they determine perception. When you possess two (or more) viewpoints, you can achieve a sort of binocular vision. In the same way that two eyes give you depth of field, so two cultures give you depth of meaning.

What one learns in doing fieldwork *always* highlights the fact that your earlier ways of seeing or doing were culture-bound. In the middle 1960s I worked in the Bay Area of San Francisco, studying Americans who were getting divorced. I learned how difficult it is for some people to alter the culture they already know. Norman Mailer once said that being married to two different women is like living in two different countries. He was right, and the point is equally true for women who marry different men. The point is, some people adapt easily and well to one of such "foreign" countries. A few can become positively cosmopolitan—as in polygamy. And another few can't make the adjustment at all.

Fieldworkers also learn that people (including themselves) are not aware that they have cultural expectations until those expectations are not being met. My divorce research showed that it was easier for some people to blame their spouses than to learn new ways.

Later, when doing fieldwork among stepfamilies in the United States, I interviewed a number of adults who had acquired stepfathers when they were children. One of my standard questions was, "What occurs to you most vividly when you think about being a stepchild?" I was not prepared for the frequent answer: "That *awful* food!" For example, one man's biological father was a fussy eater of refined vegetarian foods. His stepfather was a meat-and-potatoes man. The family diet changed because wives were supposed to cook for their husbands, and kids were supposed to eat whatever was put in front of them. Almost surely the mothers never realized that changing something as homely and habituated as family meals could be an ordeal for their children when the "father" changed.

The point of all this is that culture is made up of many little things—all easily understood, all human. Many of those little things, especially those from the ethnographer's own culture, never make it into the books or even into the field notes. But when you stack them up—especially if there are differences in what people have to do to make a living, differences in their ideas about God, differences in their ideas about power in social relations and the power of the state or the church—you begin to see that some of those ideas have become "values" that *do* make a difference. People may just not be willing to pay what it would cost them to give up "the way things are supposed to be."

This is always a chastening experience. At the same time, being chastened in that way makes you a more complete human being. Human beings can choose—indeed, they *have* to choose. Having made a choice, they often encounter great difficulty in going back to alter it. Human beings, we repeat, learn to be provincial at the same time that they learn to be fully human.

Those small provincialisms can be deadly. In Northern Ireland or Bosnia in the 1990s, about the only difference between the people of the warring factions is religion. The Balkans' Serbs and Croats and Bosnians speak the same language and have, except for religion, the same culture. The major difference is that Serbs are brought up to hate Roman Catholic Croats, and Croats are brought up to hate Greek Orthodox Serbs, and both hate the Muslim Bosnians.

In North America and many parts of Europe, ethnic problems arise because many people associate similar but functionally irrelevant cultural differences with the economic and political relations among ethnic groups. Minor distinctions are given special meaning and used as proof that "other" people are not just different but inferior. Moreover, we confuse ethnic culture with race. In fact, race and culture are absolutely distinct and separable attributes. Any normal child can learn any culture, any language, but *usually* it cannot learn to be of another race. The exceptions exist because race is not really a biological category but a cultural one. There have always been people of mixed ethnic heritages who "passed" as members of one category or the other—usually the dominant category. Some people with both African and Caucasian ancestors can readily pass for White. More interestingly, some individuals with as many as seven Caucasians among their eight great-grandparents have suddenly realized they were Indians—that is especially true of those who seek to activate membership in a tribe that has done well with casinos. They discover roots they had forgotten. But this phenomenon is not restricted to race. In India, some people born in scheduled castes have claimed to be Untouchables, to make themselves eligible for special scholarships.

Given the fact that today we all live in a global culture, provincialism gets us in trouble more and more easily. It gets governments in trouble. It gets businesses in trouble. And *that* makes ethnography increasingly important.

We have entered an era so fraught with potential for mass-destruction that we must learn to think and act in terms of the entire human species, not just our local part of it. If we don't, we will kill each other in ever-greater numbers about things that don't matter to survival or happiness. With six billion of us and growing, we need ethnography more than ever to make us comprehend and appreciate our common humanity.

Chapter Twelve

Does Ethnography
Falsify Reality?

Culture is a set of ongoing processes; there are no natural borders within or between cultures. All human societies have culture, but it is a necessary part of their self-consciousness to distinguish their version from every other. "A culture" is thus a common understanding, not an objective reality. In explaining how culture is "done" locally, ethnographers have to accept that any ethnography, like a snapshot, turns a process into a static record of what existed and occurred at a particular time and place.

In North America, ethnography began with studies of those who peopled the New World before Westerners arrived. The context of early observations included a painful awareness that the indigenous cultures had been knocked askew by the movements of European immigrants, freed slaves of African descent, and the Amerindians themselves. The First Americans were still being decimated by alien diseases and the policies of various national governments, and the survivors were turned into encapsulated minorities.

The early ethnographers set out to learn and describe what pre-Contact cultures had been like before they were hit by the Euro-American juggernaut. Unfortunately they had, especially in the beginning, a terribly simplistic view of culture: they assumed all non-Western lifeways were necessarily stable until "disturbed." At that early date, no one yet realized that *all* societies are *always* in a state of change. Sometimes the pace of change is fast, sometimes slow, but as long as people die and are replaced, and as long as they keep having ideas, culture will change.

To "recover" that imaginary static state, the early ethnographers interviewed old men (and, less often, old women) who remembered "the good old days"—overlooking the fact that the attitudes and memories of the elderly, like everybody else's, are influenced by everything that has happened to them since the events in question occurred.

The memories of old people are, of course, immensely valuable to understanding any culture—if we remember that culture is an ongoing process and that they are telling you what they *now* think happened *then*. Memories reflect our views of the present and the past, and they certainly affect our views of the future. Myths and legends often contain references to events that archaeology or history can substantiate. But to assume that memories can provide a factually accurate picture of the past is naive at best—here we run into the eyewitness problem again. Early ethnographers did indeed leave us much valuable information, but their basic assumptions about culture history do not stand up.

Culture is *not* a *thing*. As it goes on—in a constantly progressing Present that links a Past with a Future—it is a set of complicated processes. (Many ethnographers fail to report or even indicate an awareness of the processes because they may not show up in the course of a year's fieldwork.) Moreover, every person who uses "the same" culture knows and operates a slightly different aspect of it. Your America—or Europe or Asia—is not the same as your neighbor's, or ours. As an ethnographer you must consider just who it was that told you what—the personal history of that person, and what the person had to gain or lose by reporting it. Furthermore, you must always remember that people have different kinds of experiences and will therefore have different opinions about the same issue.

There is an even deeper problem. When people's words and works are recorded, they become static. Ethnography, like a snapshot, freezes a moment. Every photograph is indeed a glimpse of truth, but the full truth comes out only when you remember that there was a before and an after for each photograph. Real life is *never* static, but written or photographed ethnography *always* is. Life goes on after ethnography, just as it does after the snapshot is taken. Moving pictures don't alter that snapshot quality; ethnographic reporting has included movies ever since film was invented.

Succeeding scholars provide more such photographs. When there are several ethnographers, we are offered snapshots taken at different times, with different cameras, from different angles or perspectives. Sometimes they may seem to contradict one another; usually that indicates nothing more than that we haven't hooked the photographs together in a sensible historical sequence; occasionally it indicates that different ethnographers focused on different details. But it can happen that two ethnographers actually disagree on the meaning of what they saw (as Mead and Freeman did).

Because of these difficulties, some anthropologists have gone so far as to call all written ethnography "fiction." It isn't, of course. Any ethnographer, like any photographer, can be second-guessed: Why did you record this but not that; why did you start here and stop there? The point is that a record exists, and we can examine it. When we consider what any fieldworker wrote, we must remember that *all* ethnographers are limited by their own culture—including whatever anthropological culture they have learned. We are all limited by our particular abilities and convictions, by the perceptions and values instilled into us.

Thus, no ethnography is ever a "true" and "complete" picture of "the" culture. It is wrong-headed to assume that the static quality in a published report reflects some static quality in the culture itself. Cultures change, all the time. They change when we are not present, they change while we are there. They even change just *because* we are there! I vividly remember walking down a path in Tivland in Africa one bright morning and hearing somebody whistle the opening bars of Brahms's Fourth Symphony. Startled, I went to check it out. It turned out to be a man I knew. "Where did you learn that?" I asked him. His answer surprised me again but in a different way: "From you!"

It is not disagreement among ethnographers working at different times that ought to make us suspicious, but their total consensus. *That* would indicate collusion or censorship!

As late as the 1940s, efforts were still being made to record traditional Native American culture "before it disappears." It was easy to ignore the fact that Indians were necessarily adapting and changing *before* the arrival of European and African immigrants. But they were, because every population uses in its daily lives some combination of old and new ideas to produce ever-newer ones. There never has been a stable "before" to which you can compare the present: every culture is always undergoing drift and change, at times very slow, at times very fast.

Recovering past culture is a worthy pursuit—*if* you remember the traps that await you. Those traps become evident when you think about what we humans have physically inherited from ancestors as close to us as the people who lived by hunting and gathering. The biology of our digestion today comes from those forebears' adjustment to *their* environment. They ate lots of vegetable fiber, very little in the way of fats and even less in the way of sugars. The bodies we inherit from them evolved, over eons, to make us like the taste of scarce fats and sweets. Today, when both are ubiquitous and cheap, we need to make a conscious adjustment to curb our Paleolithic appetites. Many of us find that isn't easy.

It is debatable whether there are any hunters and gatherers left who can be meaningfully compared to those ancestors, but their cultural inheritance still affects us. Native Alaskans, for example, are by law allotted special hunting and fishing rights beyond the privileges of other citizens of that state. The Alaskan legislature and its Department of Fish and Game agree that Native Alaskans have what they call "subsistence rights" because it is "their culture." Although historically the ancestors of today's Native Alaskans did indeed subsist as hunters and gatherers, and although many of them still fish and hunt some meat and gather some plants, what the law actually does is set them apart from Alaska's other citizens. It dictates that some people have rights that others would also like but do not have. Native Alaskan culture today includes (in addition to the right to fish and hunt out of season) government-supported schools, modern corporations into which tribal members have organized themselves, and salaried work for oil companies. It also includes snowmobiles and canned foods, kerosene and television, Guns-and-Roses T-shirts, and a lot of other stuff that they share with the other North Americans living all around them. Many Native Alaskans buy expensive fishing boats and sell their catch in Seattle. Their situation is far from unique; native peoples in British Columbia and other Canadian provinces undergo similar acculturative experiences. So, with local variations, do the peoples who live on reservations in the western United States. Their political *apartheid*—a special legal position based on the myth of their historical culture—helps them maintain an identity that they value. Please note that we did *not* say that they shouldn't have it.

Another example: in the late 1950s an ethnographer named Colin Turnbull studied the pygmies of the Ituri Forest in what was then called the Belgian Congo but became Zaire and is at this writing called The Democratic Republic of Congo. Turnbull wrote a fine ethnography about what was going on among pygmies at that time. He gave good coverage to the fact that they were in touch with Bantu peoples of different cultures who lived near them. But he paid almost no attention to the fact that, at the time of his fieldwork, Belgian officials were not only present but were consciously changing and directing the cultures of both Bantu and pygmy.

But we have just introduced another problem—again a problem with definition, not with the "facts." The classification "hunters and gatherers" or "food collectors" was created by anthropologists. Like every other diagnostic category, it has limitations and therefore raises questions. What portion of a people's diet must come from a food-collecting economy before we can classify that people as hunters and gatherers? In the 1960s, some Caucasian northern Minnesotans got well over half their calories from food they hunted and gathered. They butchered the animals they hunted (mainly deer) and put them into their freezers. In the summer they prepared, blanched, and froze the vegetables and berries they gathered. Were these Euro-Americans "hunters and gatherers?"

How they lived is not in doubt but the category "hunter and gatherer" must be. Do I belong in it because I pick blackberries and gather wild morel mushrooms? Categories, like straightjackets, are useful and necessary only under specific conditions. What people do can be stated with some certainty, but *any* classification of behavior is necessarily limiting and full of holes and exceptions. We do indeed need categories—but we also need to beware of them, for they can trick us into not seeing what is in front of us.

This brings us back once again to asking what is "a culture" in our mixed up world? There are no natural borders between cultures. Ethnic groups can usually define which people are "Us" and which are not. But they always share some—usually many, even most—elements of their culture with neighbors who belong to another ethnic group.

What does learning about all this tell you then about facing your own day-to-day problems? That the more you know about the changes and the activities of other cultures, the better you will be able to understand and adapt to and benefit from your own.

We do indeed live in unique times—everybody always has. We live in an environment just a little different from that which our parents grew up in, one that is a great deal different from our grandparents' and increasingly different from our more distant ancestors.' Change is the only certainty. If you do not adapt, if you let yourself grow static, you perish.

If you limit yourself too strictly to what you already know—or, worse, to what your grandparents knew—you cripple your capacity to adapt, and you will find yourself in deep trouble. What some call "the eternal verities" may be useful as goals, but you have to remember that even timeless truths are expressed in ever-changing idioms. Eternal verities, expressed in varied and manifold ways, enrich your world—and each may show you a different facet of eternal truth.

Life expects you to adapt (read "change") when the environment changes. Your adaptation creates additional change in your environment. You have to keep your eye on your physical needs and limitations. It helps if you understand that there are *many* more ways to be an OK human being than the ones you have been taught. No one way is more human than any other, although some may be technologically more efficient or promote more comfortable and effective social interactions.

You have to make choices, every day. What you choose may be fatal—unless, of course, you allow yourself to change your mind and learn something, saving yourself in the process.

Ethnographers, being human, have to learn these same lessons. At the simplest level, ethnography is about what specific people do—or did, the day the data were gathered. But at another level, of course, all ethnography is about all of us.

Chapter Thirteen

Beyond Academe

Good ethnography can be and has been done by nonanthropologists, although anthropological training will make it easier. Every account should include information about the ethnographer's training, reactions, misgivings, and musings.

Since about 1910, some academic anthropologists have claimed that reliable information can be collected only by what they call "trained observers," by which they mean *anthropologically* trained observers. Could it be that they were wrong about that? Is *everything* outside their purview really untrustworthy? Could their objection stem from nothing more than that material collected by nonanthropologists is sometimes organized along different lines, in order to serve different purposes? What *does* qualify an observer? How do you learn what you have to know to do this job?

People who do not identify themselves as anthropologists can collect and report valuable ethnographic information. Edmund Wilson was an essayist, a literary critic and student of world literature—the kind of man who, when he was already an elder, learned Hungarian so that he could read the works of Joseph Leyel in the original. Wilson generally despised academics. His *With Apologies To The Iroquois* may be a better description of these Native Americans, their history, and their vicissitudes in adapting to the Europeans than any anthropological ethnographer has written, and some of theirs are pretty good. Wilson prepared himself so well for this book, reading every anthropological ethnography and everything else written about the Iroquois, that some anthropologists have called him a "self-educated anthropologist." They mean it as a compliment, but he might well have resented it; he was that sort of man.

Elizabeth Marshall Thomas, who wrote *The Harmless People*, an important book about the Bushmen of South Africa, offers a different sort of example. She knew a lot of anthropology—her mother Lorna Marshall and her brother John Marshall both became anthropologists who studied the Bushmen. Lorna's articles are among the most revealing ever published about these interesting people; John's films are classics. Elizabeth chose a different literary form. *The Harmless People* used careful observation, and its facts are accurate by stringent standards, but they are *not* arranged to cater to academic theories; she sought—and found—a broader audience. She used story for its own sake, instead of pigeonholing her information within the standard categories of kinship, economics, religion, and so forth. What she wrote amounts to a new kind of travel book, one that presents a more informed context, suitable for an era in which pleasure-travelers seek something exotic or unusual. Her nonanthropological readers can actually imagine themselves seeing what she reported.

A second type of nonanthropological ethnographer has emerged and also demands special attention. We mean the educated descendants of the subjects of ethnographic study. The culture of their parents and grandparents is of interest to them, and they probably think of it as their own. But they may consider the ethnographic record as full of mistakes where it is not like the culture that they themselves experienced. Part of that may be anthropological "error," but much of it is difference in point of view and how the sweep of history has changed what they experienced from what their grandparents experienced. This topic needs careful study.

Some New Guineans today don more-or-less traditional paint to perform more-or-less traditional dances for tourists. But when the tourists are gone, these same people work for wages, run their own government and businesses, and study their homework. Some Native Americans welcome tourists to their powwows, in which traditional and modern dances are performed not only for themselves but for the tourists' edification and cash. Throughout much of Africa you can buy "airport art," which a derisive term for "bad" copies of old art forms. It is better if we can learn to see it not as "bad art" by comparison with the traditional, but rather as new versions of traditional culture that are being recast as a commodity and sold for a profit.

This leads to two important questions. The first, "What is genuine ethnography?", is difficult to answer. Because all ethnography has to pass through the mind of the person who writes it down, the idea of genuineness may not be valid here, even though we know that some ethnographers made mistakes because they did not understand what they were told.

The second question, "What is meant by 'true' presentation of ethnographic facts?", concerns *how* the work is done. Again, context is crucial. That airport art is sure-enough real culture. To dismiss it as mere "debasement" of some traditional "true" culture is to disregard the context in which people are living. Airport art results from a demand created by the market, rather than one created by religious beliefs. That the market is less demanding of skill and beauty than the supernaturals were is not a condemnation, but a fact.

Bad ethnography, no matter who does it, results from poor fieldwork (which usually results from superficiality in looking and asking, or from not listening carefully). The problem almost always begins when personal convictions prevent understanding—or even seeing and hearing—what is going on. We think that purposeful falsification of ethnography is rare, even though we know that Evans-Pritchard, in the Sudan, fobbed off a whole phoney ethnography on a man he considered a phoney. The man later convicted himself as a plagiarist and a fool when he published it, to E-P's delight, as "ethnography."

Chapter Fourteen

Culture Shock

Your learning experience in reading ethnographies includes the discomfort you may experience in finding yourself understanding behaviors resulting logically from premises alien to your own culture.

Anthropological training will sharpen a person's skills for doing fieldwork. However, no amount of academic preparation can equip you to look into yourself and become aware that you have cultural limitations. When an alien logic penetrates, when your habituated convictions and values are knocked into a cocked hat, the agitation you feel is called culture shock. Your capacity to predict what might happen has "turned" on you—you feel it as a threat to your very existence. Training may warn you to expect to experience it. But training can never tell you how to deal with it when it actually happens. Only on-the-job training lets you meet the moment and master it—if you are secure and "together" enough. You may even master it—and get pretty good at it.

You can probably *never* tell when you are *not* achieving sufficient mastery over your own values and prejudices to allow yourself to deal with information of the sort which forces you to question your own culture's basic assumptions. Culture shock, however, *sometimes* tells when you *are* doing it. You may be devastated, you may be "converted," you may be outraged! You may insist that you weren't raised to tolerate this crap, you may trumpet your superiority to "their" way of thinking or acting. You may even deny being affected by it.

I still remember vividly the evening, among the Tiv in Nigeria, when my Tiv assistant (who could write the Tiv language, but knew almost no English) came to announce that he was back from the river, where he had gone to bathe. He noted casually that a man had drowned while he was there. The man was a stranger, he said, and did not know there was a sudden drop of the river bottom when you got out about ten feet. He stepped off that drop, could not swim, and drowned. "Didn't anybody try to save him?" He said they did not. I knew him to be a strong swimmer—"Didn't *you* try to save him?" The answer: "He wasn't mine."

I learned things about one of my own deepest values that night: that my idea about "my" people was defined very differently from his definition of "my" people. That, indeed, I had at least half-a-dozen contexts of just who "my" people were, and what my responsibilities were, and that they changed from one context to another. His ideas were quite—well, different. Involuntarily, I despised him and all his people; it took me a day or two to adjust to our differences. Where, I asked myself, was their common humanity? And where, I was forced to ask myself a day or so later, did I get the idea that I should be responsible for humanity?

Some people give up and go home when this sort of thing happens to them. Others go "native." And still others come painfully to realize that they themselves have values that outsiders consider weird.

The key to getting through culture shock is to be found in your response: if you can admit that you are experiencing an irrational and mindlessly emotional reaction, you have a chance to think your way through it. You can begin to ask, again, how this new data meshes with everything else you know. But you *do* have to find a new balance. It isn't always easy—but it *is* always rewarding.

Good ethnographers tell readers about their backgrounds, their convictions, their culture shock. Those are part of the story. There are risks here too—you may fall into the "Oh, boy, did I suffer!" error. But even that is better than the "phoney-contribution error," in which an occasional ethnographer reinforces cast-iron ego-defenses so cleverly that it comes out as pseudotheory. Such an ethnographer has avoided dealing with culture shock. The reader has been mislead.

As consumers of ethnography, readers can also suffer culture shock, although readers are less vulnerable than fieldworkers. Readers can always just ignore some paragraphs; they can close the book and never open it again; they can kid themselves that it isn't really shocking but just boring. Still, if you do close that book, remember that boredom may be a defensive reaction against disturbing material—you can hide your revulsion by turning it into boredom (we agree, of course, that some writers actually *are* boring). Make sure that the trouble really is "out there" in the book and not "in here" in yourself. It is, after all, extremely difficult to tell when intellectual cowardice is limiting you.

Whether you are researching it or reading it, ethnography necessarily demands, as we mentioned in chapter 6, both a systematic examination of what is happening in a strange society *and* a simultaneous exploration of what is happening to yourself. Naturally, reading and using an ethnography are not as hard as creating one. After all, as a reader you are not alone in the dark, sweating existential bullets among aliens in some place your parents never heard of. But it *does* require some of the same discipline if you are going to deal with it successfully. When you come across something mindboggling in an ethnography, your first (and totally natural) reaction is to consider "them" ignorant, benighted, and stupid. It may, at times, be hard to remember that what you are reading is a description of a lifeway that has *worked* for somebody! You have to be willing to admit that there are aspects of the human experience about which you know very little—that you have much to learn. You can learn a lot of it by allowing yourself to experience the weightlessness that comes when your sense of cultural gravity is knocked out—when you are forced to reorganize your thinking so that you can continue to function as *you*. You have to remind yourself that your purpose in reading ethnography is to expand your horizons, which cannot be done if you hide behind mental walls that imprison you in your own private provincialism.

Actually, of course, reading ethnographies cannot possibly hurt you, for the simple reason that you remain in control. But it can make you uncomfortable when the new information raises doubts about your own way of life—even unconscious doubts that make you uncomfortable but don't tell you why.

One of the purposes of ethnography is to make you realize that your own cultural ways are limited—and maybe not as good and just and inevitable as you once thought they were. Learning that can be painful. But *not* learning it is suicide by ossification.

Chapter Fifteen

The Aliens Next Door

---

*Systematic ethnography began among peoples whose cultural ways dif-
fered widely from their ethnographers.' But cultural differences can also
be found close to home; you can do good ethnography down the block. For
today's complex societies to work even moderately well, we need to understand the cultural differences among their many composite groups, who
may not know much about one another.*

Traditionally, anthropological ethnographers preferred to work among
people who lived far away, under conditions that could be considered severe.
We call this yearning for danger and hardship in faraway places a "Masai complex," after the much admired warrior-herders of East Africa. The Masai complex means that the more perilous and remote your fieldwork, the higher you
rank among your peers. For too long, the Masai complex kept us from looking
at the strangers who live nearby, speak our language, and seem "ordinary."

I remember one student at Northwestern University, a young woman
from Wisconsin, who was doing her practice-teaching in a Chicago suburb with
a large middle-class Jewish population. One of her assignments was to oversee
a late-afternoon study hall. She had trouble keeping order in that room, but
not in other contexts. When she reported her frustration to a seminar in the
School of Education, I suggested she ask the students why she was having
trouble. At our next session she turned up elated: keeping order was still difficult, she said, but now she knew *why* pandemonium reigned in that room. And
it was not her fault! The students had told her, when she asked, that their parents insisted that the kids work at getting a good education, but equated getting an education with doing homework. "If we do it in study hall, we won't
have any to take home with us, and our parents will call you up and say you
aren't working us hard enough!" A Wisconsin Lutheran teacher had, in her
own view, learned something from and about Jewish kids in Skokie. *That* is
what ethnography is about!

55

People's actions usually make sense *if you can manage to see what they see* in the world around them. It helps more than anything else if you just *ask* them.

Anthropologist Eliot Liebow, who was White, began to hang around a street corner with a group of Black men in Washington, D.C. They eventually accepted him. He started to understand why they hung around there, and that led him to grasp some of the many problems that beset poor young men in Black communities. He made an important contribution to ethnography in his *Talley's Corner.* Street corner hangers in Washington, D.C., have undoubtedly changed a lot since the 1950s, when Liebow made his inquiries and did his fieldwork. Then, they didn't have guns, and there was almost no drug trade. We don't know much about them as they are today—there has not yet been a second Eliot Liebow.

In the 1960s anthropologist R. Lincoln Keiser, another young White man, hung with a "delinquent gang" of Chicago's ghetto Blacks and was allowed to research and write *The Vice Lords*, a history and description of their gang and the larger federation of Black gangs of which it was part.

In the 1970s, Michael Agar published some riveting studies about addicts, pushers, and their street culture.

Although Liebow, Keiser, and Agar did magnificent ethnography and certainly proved their personal courage, their studies seem almost innocent now, decades later, against the backdrop of violence in the very communities where they once pursued fieldwork.

The White middle class also offers opportunities to an ethnographer. As mentioned previously, I did a study of divorcing middle-class people in the Bay area of California (also in the 1960s). In order to get divorced in those days, you had to prove in court that your spouse was guilty of some transgression that lawmakers had specifically made acceptable as grounds for divorce: transgressions like physical abuse, adultery, or failure to support. Divorce then was still considered a sign of personal failure; many divorcees reported that they were isolated by their former communities. When I repeated that study in 1980, the stigma was not as great; the feeling of failure was not as severe; the law was more sensible; the lawyers, detectives, social workers and therapists' jobs had changed. Everything had changed except two facts: divorce is a miserable experience and everybody is still worried about the children.

Then as now, divorce altered the contexts in which people lived. The single-again found themselves in a community of divorcees, having to learn a lot of culture that was new to them because it had evolved outside the realm of the undivorced.

Although much was known about divorce in the 1960s, information about the subject was compartmentalized. Lawyers, therapists, clergymen, social workers, and detectives had each created large literatures. However, since none of them ever read any of it but their own, there was no general overview. An ethnographic angle on the processes of marriage-dissolution brought all the compartments together into a single context. We interviewed people who were undergoing divorce about what was happening to them; before that time, psychiatrists and social workers had been the only people who even *tried* to get information from divorcees about their experiences, and their purpose was to help the divorcees adjust, not to make a contribution to behavioral science.

The ethnographic method turns out to be fairly easy to describe, and it works on local problems and among neighbors just as well as it does among distant and romantic Exotics. There used to be an old Cadillac ad that advised you to "Ask the man who owns one." That is what ethnographers do: they ask the person who "owns one." The answers provide us with a mass of edifying, yet fairly simple, information. That just *may* settle a lot of problems.

Some individuals say they are embarrassed to question others—that they are afraid they are "intruding." They use elaborate (and learned) cultural notions about privacy as an excuse for doing nothing. Rest assured that if you actually are intruding, those you're imposing on will let you know. Very quickly. It is astonishing, however, how many of the people whom you *did* ask end up telling you far more than you asked for—more even than you want to know—and then add that they are grateful for your questions. They say that you gave them an opportunity to summarize their experiences. Even more important to many of them, you allowed them to feel as if their difficult experiences could be helpful to others.

One warning: since the 1970s there has been a spate of legal and bureaucratic obstacles put in the way of doing the kind of research we are talking about here. Today's university research committees have codes of ethics which insist that all human "subjects" sign "informed consent" forms before you can ask them questions. It has come to the point, some anthropologists complain that "today, only journalists can do classical anthropological fieldwork with impunity." That is a very real problem—one that grew out of a total misunderstanding of what ethnography involves. Ethnography does not hurt the people whom you ask for information. It may be true that some of that information might be used against the people who provide it—but *not* if the ethnographer is ethical and sensible.

Learning to ask questions of your neighbors and of the people you work with, and doing it tactfully, can foster mutual respect and understanding; it can clear the air. It can save you from a lot of the pain and misunderstanding that come from ignorance and supposition.

Chapter Sixteen

The Collapse of Colonialism

The most recent bout of colonialism—a political system in which great powers turn lesser social systems into dependencies—ended around 1960. The British, Dutch, and French empires dissolved at that time, as the Spanish, German, Italian, and American empires had done earlier, and the Portuguese and Russian ones did a little later. With the end of empire, ethnographers came to realize that they had reported not indigenous culture, but one part of colonial culture.

World events and the forces they portend have an impact on the way we look at ethnography. One of the most important developments in the mid-twentieth century was that colonialism disappeared. Colonies are as old as history: one group conquers another and turns it into a dependency. Or emigrants leave a country, found a settlement in some new place, bring their culture with them, and maintain ties with the "old country."

In recent centuries there have been two major colonialist movements by the Western world. The first began five centuries ago, when the kings of Portugal and Spain received papal authority to spread Christianity by establishing colonies in Africa, Asia, and the New World. In order to understand that quest, we have to realize that in mercantilism (their precapitalist economic system) taxation was almost nonexistent. Kings controlled imports and exports; they got their resources from trade, conquest, and exploration in search of valuables. And they always needed money to pay for the wars which are the *sine qua non* of feudalism.

The Iberian kings' missionary urge was partly a dodge to get the Pope's approval. Without it, it would have been almost impossible to get men to risk life and limb under the intolerable conditions of travel in those days. The monarchs were interested primarily in gold, jewels, and spices. Colonies were essential as sources of such raw materials; the wealth derived from them (particularly precious metals) went straight into their coffers.

The Spaniards and Portuguese were soon joined by their enemies the Dutch, the French, and the British. The founding of the colonies that would evolve into the United States and Canada was part of this colonial movement. Remnants of French colonial efforts in the New World can be found in Quebec, Louisiana, French Guiana, and some Caribbean islands. Dutch is still the official language of Suriname (which the Dutch got from the British by trading away what is now New York) and some of the Windward and Leeward Islands. Latin Americans still speak Spanish or Portuguese, their architecture still reflects the style of those colonial powers, and most people there are still Roman Catholics.

Colonization of India by the French and English, and of Indonesia by the Dutch, occurred in the same period. For nearly a century, Holland dominated the West African slave trade. Russia's empire expanded primarily over land: south first into the Caucasus and then against Turkey and other Islamic countries of the Near East; east across Siberia to the Pacific Ocean and then into Alaska and along North America's west coast into what is now called California.

The American revolution was an early success in the growing resistance to this surge of colonialism. Other parts of the European empires, especially in India and Indonesia, persisted until after World War II. The Russian empire did not collapse until 1989. Even now, the European Union includes some territories in the Caribbean and the Indian Ocean which are still considered part of France.

The second major colonial surge occurred during the 1800s. This one was founded not on mercantilism but on the capitalist principles that emerged with the Industrial Revolution. At the end of the nineteenth century, Britain, France, Belgium, and Germany divided up Africa. They established colonial governments whose authorities, from the start, considered the people they ruled to be culturally and morally inferior. The British came to call the situation, in Rudyard Kipling's phrase, "the White man's burden."

This second surge of colonialism had a far greater impact on ethnography than the earlier one which had occurred before specialized and thorough ethnography was even imagined (although works like Sahagun's exhaustive description of the Aztecs came from the first period). During this rebirth of colonialism, governments and private interests were eager to understand the lifeways and values of the people whose territories they controlled—the better to profit from them. Especially in Great Britain and the Netherlands, ethnographic research was encouraged as an official function of colonialism.

Until the 1950s, a great many English, Dutch, and French anthropologists were employed by their respective foreign and colonial offices. Most of the individuals who actually went out to live with the "natives," to learn how and why they did things, hoped their work would enable colonial administrators to rule the locals with fewer misunderstandings—and certainly with less need for military intervention. They believed, probably correctly in most cases, that their efforts minimized the destruction of local cultures.

It is fair to say that ethnography, especially in Europe, came of age, not in reporting on the locally-varied traditional world that its practitioners thought they were describing, but on a "Third World" transformed (if not quite created) by the efforts of imperial powers. It does as little good to curse anthropology for its colonial past as it does to curse medicine for at one time bleeding the sick. In spite of their cultural blinders, these early ethnographers helped redirect attitudes within the colonizing nations so as to encourage the tide of independence that swept their colonies in the 1950s and '60s.

In North America meanwhile, most anthropological work was carried out among the First Americans who, by the time they were studied, resided for the most part on reservations. A comparison of colonialism and reservation policy is instructive: both imposed a culture to which the "natives" had to adjust.

When first India and then the African and Indonesian colonies became independent nations (from the 1940s into the 1960s), an important truth stood revealed. Ethnographers had been writing reports with *far* too little reference to the colonizing power. Too seldom did they consider the impact of the peace imposed by colonial troops. They may have mentioned, but almost never investigated, the power of colonial administrators over social relations among the various segments of the population. For example, the British colonial administration of Nigeria came to the conclusion that the Tiv method of exchange marriage was so complicated that they, the British, could never understand it and hence administer justice under it—so they legally banned it. Can you imagine what it would mean if our own marriage traditions were suddenly legally abolished? That same British administration said that, because witchcraft was a fiction, they could not allow any cases involving witchcraft to enter the courts. In order to settle disputes involving beliefs that the British could not understand, the Tiv therefore had to set up what the British called "kangaroo courts."

Ethnographers dutifully noted that colonial governments required taxes from their subject peoples, but the connection between taxes and the introduction of money with which to pay them was not given as much attention as it deserved. Laws imposed by the Westerners interfered at many levels with the ways people had traditionally lived.

These factors and others suddenly became evident when the colonial powers "extended freedom" to the colonies and went home. Ethnographers, who'd had difficulty seeing how deeply the colonial overlay had impacted the locals, were suddenly forced to reconsider what they had observed and described earlier. The same thing happened with our understanding of Native Americans: they too had been subjected to an earlier colonial culture, and they too still bear its marks.

One side-effect of the end of colonialism is that it exposed what we now think of as its immorality. Anthropologists had to ask themselves, "Were *we* part of this corruption? Were *we* in part responsible for what we now see as the degradation of colonized peoples?" *Why* had they been collecting this information? Had they been unconscious tools of colonialism? Were they still doing something that could disadvantage the people they were studying?

The war in Vietnam sharpened this debate within the anthropological community in the United States. Could *any* anthropologist, could you, in good conscience, give out information about the people you had once lived with, befriended and studied, knowing that the U.S. armed forces might employ it for targeting purposes? Even if it "saved American lives?" Who should merit your primary loyalty: your nation, your employer, or the native people whose guest you were?

These were not easy questions to answer. They restructured the moral basis of ethnography's changing context. New ethical guidelines emerged. The prime directive for fieldworkers became the same as that for doctors: *First, do no harm.*

In one case which drew international attention, an American anthropologist was denied a doctorate at Stanford University because he had embarrassed his host society with information he had collected on his fieldwork. After he had left Mainland China as one of the first Americans allowed to do research there, he chose to express his disapproval of China's population policies by publishing—in Taiwanese newspapers, which made it even worse to the Mainland Chinese—stories and photographs of women selected to undergo forced abortions. Not only did he compromise every other anthropologist then doing fieldwork in the Peoples Republic, he put at risk the clearly identifiable individuals in these photographs. The university (and the discipline) concluded that he had no right to risk the privacy of his informants just because his personal morality conflicted with that of the government of the people he was studying. In our terms: he had dealt with his culture shock in an unprofessional manner.

Ethnography has survived the ending of the second period of colonialism even though much of its traditional "field" disappeared. Ethnography continues—and continues to improve in quality. But anthropology and its theoretical stance find themselves at a crossroad. New philosophies have emerged; so has global culture. To whom and what do we turn for direction?

We believe that anthropology will be safe as long as the quality of ethnography continues to flourish. However, there are *a lot* of ideas to sort out if we are to get the most out of all that fieldwork.

Chapter Seventeen

Who Speaks for Whom?

The demise of colonialism gave rise to moral issues like human rights and political hegemony. The basic questions turn out to be: does any people have a right to claim that their own view of themselves is the only legitimate view? Can culture be "owned"? Do ethnographers actually rip off the people they study?

Since the collapse of colonialism, a growing body of scholars has emerged in the newly independent nations. Many of them are trained so that their view of their own people and their history stands alongside the views of specialists from other cultures. They sometimes disapprove of what those foreign ethnographers have written. Some even claim that nobody but themselves should be allowed to speak for their people—thereby guaranteeing that their own distortions will be the only distortions available.

For example, during most of this century the races in South Africa were ranked by a system called *apartheid* (separateness), which classified every inhabitant as either White, Colored, Black, or Other (Indians, Orientals) in a legally enforced and often lethally brutal inequality which benefitted the White minority at the cost of everybody else. Before the end of apartheid in June, 1991, White South Africans would tell you that there was no way that any person who was not South African (they did not say it, but they meant White South African) could understand the suffering of both Blacks and Whites in their nation. Their underlying message was that the intellectual understanding of outsiders was inadequate because it did not incorporate the emotional understanding that insiders brought to it.

Insider views always carry a heavy emotional ingredient—and may be almost devoid of any intellectual component. Insiders, it must be faced, have something to prove. Outsider views, on the other hand, are largely intellectualized; if they contain any emotional content at all, it is generally rooted in a totally different context.

Insider views in any culture are likely to be short-sighted because insiders are blinded by emotions, especially if they cannot figure out ways to improve their position. Outsider views may be inept because the outsider either sees the situation as "mere facts" or else is blinded by quite different (and possibly inappropriate) emotions. Consider, for example, Israelis and Palestinians, or Protestant and Catholic Irish, and the outside world's inability to affect their postures.

The moral is obvious: the emotional dimensions in an ethnography, if not openly discussed, will cloud the issues. Good ethnographers therefore admit their outsider status and try to present their outside view as best they can while also reporting the inside view and the emotions which surround it. Any outside view presented *without* the emotion of the participant observer will draw resentment: insiders will insist that the outsider doesn't "understand."

Among First Americans and African Americans in the 1990s, this problem is often expressed as a conviction that Whitey not only *does not* understand but that Whitey *cannot* understand their suffering, or their fury. In truth, Whites in North America may well be ignorant of, or at least foreign to, the emotions that those groups attach to their historical experience and their suffering. A few Whites may even be unsympathetic. But *if* Whites allow themselves to be educated in those matters, they *can* understand.

These insider-outsider factors sometimes get mixed up with the idea that a culture is the private property of the people who were raised in it. Native Americans have expressed resentment at archaeologists and ethnographers for "making money" from studying their culture. What they *really* resent may well be that these outsiders, though they came to understand the Indians' problems, haven't been able to correct the inequities. "They come here, they take our way of life and make money with it. Then they leave us just as miserable and poor as we were before they came. And we get nothing!"

Ideas of exploitation may even get mixed up with conspiracy theory. The disadvantaged say: if you can understand our predicament, how come you don't fix it? And then they brand the ethnographer as part of the conspiracy which keeps them marginal.

Ethnographers themselves are sometimes led astray by this. Learning somebody else's culture and putting out the good word is *not* exploitation. Not even if the author of the good word makes a modest living doing so. Nevertheless, some anthropologists have taken the position that whatever money comes to them as a result of having done the study should be given to the people who provided the information. Whether in any particular case this is a fine or a foolish thing, it is a moral problem. How you handle it depends on whether you believe that the culture you described is the "property" of the people from whom you learned it. If you buy that notion, you've let ideas of exploitation get mixed up with ideas about whether culture is property, something that can be owned. Culture is not that kind of property.

Is what you learned in any class really the "property" of the professor? Of course not. Culture, which is never part of any genetic inheritance but is *always* learned, surely "belongs" to whomever masters it. If I learn French and

French culture, is it mine or theirs? I am not French. Most French people would agree that their culture is not the sole "property" of the French—indeed, the French government spends a lot of money every year trying to convince the world that French culture should be universal.

You cannot copyright a culture. You *can*, in the laws of most countries today, patent an invention or copyright a book or a piece of music so that you can be rewarded for the intellectual work you have done. This has been the basis of a dispute between the Chinese and the American governments: the Chinese do not accept the sanctity of "intellectual property" in a capitalist sense. But as it is used by ordinary people, culture does not obey *any* sort of property law. Culture is free. The moment you try to restrict who learns culture, or what they do with it, you have entered the realm of government control—indeed, of totalitarianism.

When formerly illiterate peoples learn to read what ethnographers have written about them, they may have very decided reactions. Sometimes the original ethnographic descriptions—the only record of their culture "before it all changed"—have become a sort of holy writ. (The anthropological fraternity relishes stories about fieldworkers in places like Samoa or the Trobriand Islands, who, decades after Margaret Mead, were handed her books with a dismissive: "You don't have to ask us—it's already written down.") But in other places, people may *not* like what was written about them. They may insist that the ethnographer "got it wrong."

When people say what has been written about them is wrong, it would be helpful if they clinched the point by telling what they considered to be right. It would be good of them to point out specifically what it was that the ethnographer did not understand—and perhaps suggest why he or she misunderstood it. Ethnographers are only human and therefore capable of misunderstanding. Facts can be "wrong." But if you call a fact "wrong" just because an outsider has made public some truth about your culture—especially if it is a truth that you have taken pains to keep hidden from yourselves—then your cries of "Ethnographer Error!" may get very loud, but they'll be politics, not history.

Just as ethnographers are capable of misunderstanding, informants are capable of lying. Informants may lie to you or pull your leg. The very good dictionary of the Tiv language, prepared by a colonial officer, nevertheless contains a few howlers. It gives as the Tiv name for one of the fins on the underside of the large African catfish a word that actually means "clitoris"; the fin is called something else entirely.

Probably no ethnographer can protect himself totally from this kind of informant jokes. But good ethnographers check out their facts, they get information from many sources. If there are inconsistencies in it, they are careful to find out why. A whole community cannot lie to you over an extended period of time. People may withhold the truth, but their lies will fall apart. Even the best lie will be exposed if you examine it from many points of view.

Another factor enters here: Until fairly recently, it was the convention among ethnographers to use a generalized present tense in describing the cultures and societies they reported on. This so-called "ethnographic present" has led some people to condemn an ethnography for being fifty years old, and therefore being about their grandparents rather than themselves. Even if they themselves take into account the vast changes that have taken place in the intervening years, they fear that other readers will not and that they will be perceived to be still as unenlightened or "primitive" as the people described in the ethnography.

Such a historical blindness is by no means restricted to the cultures of Others: the societies from which most ethnographers come endure the same kind of problem. For example, when the Constitution of the United States was written, the context of the society that created it was very different from what it later became. If the Constitution is to be a living document, it must be constantly reinterpreted to meet emerging conditions. Otherwise, active culture turns into dormant culture—and dormant cultures are dead cultures. When Indians (they were still called that then) were first forced onto reservations, our Constitution had a slightly different meaning than it does today; minor disparities have evolved into major injustices.

The Supreme Court has the task of keeping our Constitution current— that is, of keeping our laws within the bounds of a constantly reinterpreted charter. The Supreme Court has sometimes made what even its own Justices consider to be "mistakes." But this is a subset of another fact: We all have to work hard at keeping our culture current with the forces in our environment that impact it. And sometimes we zig when we should have zagged.

The values in a document like the Constitution are said to be eternal. But even what "eternal" means has to be constantly interpreted and reinterpreted as the here and now keeps moving on. (The "eternal flame" in cemeteries is usually kept burning for twenty years.) It is an important task to keep up with the changes that whirl around the "eternal." And every group (Democrats and Republicans, management and labor, each identifiable ethnic population, every religion) will handle the job a little differently. That is the way culture works.

Many points might be made here; we will settle for two. First, when you write ethnography, you need to establish your credibility; how else can the reader know whether you've "got it right"? One way to do this is through "reflexive ethnography." That involves a careful statement by you about how you learned these facts—the ethnocentrisms that had to be overcome and the resistance of people to talking about some matters.

Second, all culture belongs to everybody who knows it. Using it to make a profit can be legally regulated with efforts like patents and copyrights—but most culture is not copyrightable. If you learn it, it is yours. And the more you learn, the broader the expanse on which you can feel at home.

Part III

Ethnography as a Survival Mechanism

As the technology of communication gets more efficient and as airplanes get faster and cheaper, knowing the "Other" becomes more and more essential in everyone's daily life. People must know that desirable ends may be achieved in several ways—and that they will encounter those ways. They come to understand that each company—each profession—has a culture; that each legislature has a culture; that each country in the world has its own goals and its own way of seeing things. Only if we can appreciate alien ways, overcoming the difficulties to communication among many peoples, can we live constructively in the emerging world; only then will we have a better set of choices as we create our own lives.

Chapter Eighteen

The Democratization
of Ethnography

*Because World War II was carried out in places most people, including
the military, had never heard of, many anthropologists contributed to the
war effort by organizing data about people and lifeways in areas where
Americans were likely to fight. This dramatically improved the level of
knowledge about other societies. The Human Relations Area Files at Yale
University systematically organized ethnographic information and sim-
plified access. When veterans took advantage of the G.I. Bill of Rights
(government-sponsored funding for higher education) to study the social
sciences, the sudden demand for classroom materials made large-scale
ethnographic publication economically feasible.*

World War II was fought on the islands of the Pacific, in North Africa, in
many countries of Europe, East Asia and Japan. Many of those places were
known only to a few experts. The military needed to know what their forces
might encounter, what supplies could be obtained locally, and what loyalties
these far-away people might have. Anthropologists were hired to organize
whatever information existed. Unable to do fieldwork during the war, they collected and evaluated recorded information on the cultures and expectations of
every population identified as an American ally or enemy. There were, for
example, special study centers on Germany, Great Britain, Italy, Japan, Korea,
the Low Countries, and others. Most were discontinued when the war ended,
but some, like the Russian Studies Center at Harvard, still survive, as does the
Language Training Institute at Monterey.

Several first-rate books and reports came out of this era: one thinks especially of Ruth Benedict's reflection on Japanese culture, *The Chrysanthemum
and the Sword*. Benedict had never been in Japan, but she read widely and
talked to many Japanese-Americans who knew it well. From them she picked
up the values and the special ways that Japanese thought about personal

honor and the nature of society. She was instrumental in devising plans by which the Japanese, who had surrendered, could retain many of their old values as General MacArthur's Allied armies entered the country. She and her colleagues advised that the Japanese emperor be kept on his throne and used to bring about a working peace. MacArthur, to his undying credit, listened. It worked out better than anyone dared hope, and that is the prime reason why Japanese-American relations developed the sound basis they exhibit today.

One exercise in particular had a lasting effect on the way different cultures were recorded and understood. Led by anthropologists, social scientists at Yale University created a way to index references to cultural information so that it could be quickly retrieved. By today's standards it was clumsy, but at the time it was earth shattering. A faculty committee developed an index of almost 10,000 catalogable cultural items. Each was given a number. "Coders" then went through the printed records of many cultures to identify instances of those items, and assigned them code numbers. So if, for example, you wanted to know about suicide in a lot of cultures, you looked up the four-digit code for "suicide." Relevant information from many societies was then available on xeroxed pages of the original sources. Reducing information to numbers did necessarily eliminate context, but the Human Relations Area Files (HRAF) remedied that by providing a copy of the entire source so you could look up the context yourself.

HRAF led to studies that used statistics to try to prove how many societies did or did not do such and such—an updated version of what Tylor had done. These studies were informative, but not as successful as their writers had hoped. The problem was not that the data were hard to find, but that such exercises called for evaluating information by criteria not considered by the original ethnographer. It was also often impossible to know whether an instance represented one culture, or should be counted as two or more. Eventually the very concept of "*a* culture" was called into question. HRAF files did, however, make the fact inescapable that similar cultural items were often and everywhere associated with one another, like canoes and paddles, or age grading and rites of passage. HRAF, which today is totally computerized, deserves our appreciation for having furthered comparative anthropological research.

In the turbulent 1960s, especially after the Viet Nam War, student enrollment in all social science classes leaped upward. It was immediately obvious that there was nowhere near enough reading material for anthropology's new and enlarged classes. Ethnographies, the basic stuff of anthropological training, had never been mass-produced. The books were expensive and many were out of print.

Enterprising publishers began to produce special materials for the vast new crowds of consumers. Among the most successful of these ventures was a series of inexpensive ethnographic monographs edited by George and Louise Spindler. The Spindlers and their publisher made contracts with ethnographers to write student-oriented synopses of their fieldwork results. This series of short monographs—the early ones were only about 110 pages long, the later ones neared 200—eventually grew to include over 215 volumes.

This "Spindler Series" had an immense impact on the way ethnographies were reported—all good from the standpoint of students, who now had easy access to a wide range of ethnographic information. The Spindlers' success encouraged others to publish ethnographies, and so the problem of reading material for anthropology courses was solved. Many of these monographs enjoyed worldwide distribution, and some of them are still in print. People whose own parents or ancestors were described in them have actually gotten a chance to study them in school.

Professional anthropologists at that time noted, however, that the standard for an ethnographic monograph had been reduced to "a hundred pages suitable for reading by freshmen students." Today, three decades later, that once-serious objection seems trivial in light of its advantages. The woods are now full of publishers (mostly university presses) who put out ethnographic monographs, some of them very long and highly technical. Ethnographic publication has subdivided into two approaches: one suitable for teaching introductory anthropology courses, the other aimed at the ethnographer's professional colleagues.

Ethnography has been well served in the late twentieth century. Now it needs to get itself taken seriously in the world of decision makers.

Chapter Nineteen

Ethnography and Applied Anthropology

*Applied anthropology was established to overcome communication diffi-
culties among different groups of people in industry, government, or international affairs. This important administrative tool makes
ethnographic information about workers and customers accessible to decision makers, and explains managerial decisions to people who did not
participate in making them.*

Psychologists have long known that anyone who shares the opinions of
others is more comfortable than one who doesn't and that people will therefore
change their opinions in order to be part of the majority. On the other hand,
some cultures allow—and take advantage of—differences of opinion: democra-
cies have built whole political systems on the systematic expression of differences.

Nevertheless, it is astonishingly difficult to get people who take comfort
in their old ideas to listen to new ones. They may, of course, have excellent reasons for refusing to do so. In the colonial era in Africa, for example, agricultural
departments sometimes tried to introduce new crops without knowing enough
about the staple foods those crops would replace. They soon learned that a new
variety of corn might be resisted, not because the locals failed to recognize that
it produced more grain than their traditional variety, but because its timing
was out of sync with the rest of their culture. The corn they had grown up with
provided them with much-needed calories in the season before other staples
were ready for harvest; this new, "superior" corn ripened at the wrong time of
the year. The agricultural officers hadn't thought about *that*. We can call this
the "new corn trap."

The fact that traditional ideas and ways of doing things can be proved
inadequate or damaging will often seem almost irrelevant to the people who

use them—consider North Americans, cars, and public transportation for example.

A few people brand *any* new fact as ignorance or worse, no matter how convincing the proof. Some regard every innovation as evidence of a conspiracy to get their money or cause their deaths. Conspiracy theories are rife: "They" are invading us from space, "They" are unleashing genocidal new diseases. Some people still consider the theory of evolution a Satanic conspiracy, apparently without realizing that they use, every day, a lot of culture (like medicine) which only that theory could have made possible.

Developments in technology are fairly readily accepted as "improvements" *if* no change in morality is required. Changes in morality, however—even those that actually improve the condition in which people live—are far less likely to be hailed as progress. Indeed, even when such improvements are unmistakable, they may be branded as sinful. Just reflect for a moment on how changes in the traditional division of labor between men and women have been resisted even as people proceeded to take advantage of them. This is the "new morals trap."

Wherever you are, you need to be able to present new approaches and innovations in terms that will allow your audience to hear you out, or to finish reading your book. When you know what people already think, it is easier to explain new views to them—and *learning* what they think is ethnography. Knowing their views on matters that involve God, the good life, and the nature of humanity makes it easier to phrase your novel ideas so that they will be heard. But remember: only after you find out what people already believe can you hope to avoid pushing the buttons that will make them rear back, denounce you as wicked and your message as false, and refuse absolutely to consider anything new.

Applied anthropology begins with the recognition that you will have an easier time convincing people to do something in a new way if you know what their present way means to them. If you are going to get people to listen to you, to try your new product, or to cooperate with your new program and your new industrial process and organization, you'd better do the research *before* you ask them to give up what whatever it is that they know from experience works well enough. Mere efficiency won't always do.

To be accepted without pain, any change in the organization of production will need input from workers as well as managers: the workers may know a "new corn trap" the managers hadn't thought about. If management cannot convince the workers, they may have a good reason for resisting. If management can convince them, the two become allies.

To introduce new ideas or products without considering what they replace is to invite social dislocation, riots, even revolution. If you haven't done your ethnographic homework, people will almost surely resist anything you suggest to improve their lives because *your* new idea may not fit with the rest of *their* old culture. And, of course, there really may be flaws in your idea.

Some years ago, Coca-Cola's executives almost ended up with an economic disaster when they fell into the "new corn trap." They changed the fla-

vor of their product without asking the people who bought it. Habitual quaf-
fers of the stuff, some of them life-long consumers, exploded in rage. The
company was forced into a lot of expensive back-pedaling. The moral, again:
only when reinforced with knowledge from the consumers themselves will an
innovator's pitch be heard, let alone accepted, by the "natives."

Morality resists change even more violently than does taste in soft
drinks. One especially difficult institution to change is the family. Planners
often ignore the family because they forget, or never knew, that changes in *any*
institution affect the environment that families have to adjust to. Families
almost automatically take care of absolutely everything that no other institution can or does handle. "Family" is invisibly present in *all* contexts, though
often shrouded in our most enduring myths. Those myths can stultify people's
thinking: if we would just live up to our family values, they say, everything
would be fine. When President Carter set up his White House Conference on
the Family, his initial choice for heading the symposium was a divorced female
sociologist. A vocal minority instantly screamed that the fact of the woman's
divorce proved that she could not possibly know *anything* about the family, and
succeeded in getting her replaced. But who won that fine political maneuver?
Not the Republicans or the Democrats or Reason, but proponents of the
absurd myths that knowledgeable people never get divorced, that there are no
reasons good enough to justify divorce, and the most absurd myth of all: that
people who have learned a lot from experience have failed because they *had* the
experience!

People say they want families to work better, but ignorance often makes
them unwilling to listen to certain proposals that might actually help them *be*
better. Many Westerners genuinely believe that there is only one kind of family: the "nuclear" kind consisting of a mommy, a daddy and 2.3 kids; the kind
of family that they grew up in—or wish they had. They ignore single-parent
families and stepfamilies, polygynously extended families, patrilocally
extended families and all those other kinds of families that the ethnographic
record documents so richly. "Those are exceptions!" "Those are not decent!"
Period. Discussion closed.

Applied anthropologists occasionally employ two social science tech-
niques that are easy to misuse: polls and questionnaires. Polls provide information about what proportion of a population does or thinks one thing, and what
proportion another. Within our society, polls are usually conducted by telephone with a small but representative sample of respondents—which means
that on characteristics like sex, age, education, religion, ethnicity, and income,
the sample is a replica of some larger population.

In polling, the way a question is phrased almost determines the way it
will be answered. Every pollster realizes that if questions are not well stated
and well understood, any conclusions based on the answers will be at least
biased and probably misleading. Ideally, therefore, poll questions are simple
and clear, with no room for ambiguity, and answerable by a simple "Yes" or
"No." But in reality, as every teacher who's ever prepared a multiple-choice
test has learned, *ambiguity is unavoidable*. It simply isn't possible to phrase

any question, or state any declarative sentence, in such a way that it will mean the same thing to people of different cultures, social classes, or even sexes. Try it yourself; write down a meaningful college-level statement or question and let fifty people read it. You will be amazed at how outrageously misinterpreted your clearest prose can be, even by intelligent persons of good will. You may be even more dumbfounded when you are shown that this tortured reconstruction of your meaning follows logically from the words you wrote. Minds, like cultures, are predicated on premises, and we assume only at our peril that we share those of the other guy.

So what can we do to improve polling? First, admit that the questions asked are made up by the pollsters. Then, insist that the pollsters allow their respondents to criticize dumb or uninformed questions. Obviously, given the constraints they have to work under, pollsters do better if they have a sound knowledge of the people who will answer their questions. If pollsters allow statistical principles to *outweigh* ethnographic inquiry, they will end up with answers that are inaccurate and misleading. They need feedback about their questions as much as they need answers to those questions. More than that, if they get across to the people they seek to interrogate just what it is they want to know, those people can tell them *how* to ask for that information, and the results will be far more effective.

In other words, if polling is ever to become more than a statistical sledge hammer, pollsters need ethnography. And when anthropological fieldworkers poll, in the service of ethnographic data gathering, they should do so with full awareness of the limits of the technique.

Questionnaires, like polls, involve asking the opinions of representative samples of people. Though well-made questionnaires can be useful, many are ineffectual because the people who wrote the questions didn't know anything about the people who were to answer them. Again the secret is simple: *Go to the people who are to answer the questions to find out what the right questions are!*

People hold firmly to the ideas their culture underwrites as sacred or axiomatic—even, sometimes, if some of those ideas may be socially dysfunctional. Therefore, applied ethnography is essential for planned cultural change. And remember: asking merely whatever your manufacturer boss or the head of your government department wants to know can provide at best only part of the necessary information. Applied anthropologists do indeed have to find out what the boss wants to know—or else convince him that what he wants to know is more complex than originally thought. In addition, a *good* applied anthropologist has to make sure that the boss's questions will lead to useful information, by phrasing them in ways that make sense to the respondents. That is ethnography. It takes experience and sensitivity, and a certain amount of courage, to do it well.

Chapter Twenty

Ethnography in Business and Industry

The idea of ethnography has been taken up by management science and is taught in most business schools. Companies run their businesses with technical and social practices that distinguish them from other companies. In today's world, success requires you to understand not only the culture of your own company, but the cultures of those with whom it does business.

Management faculties in most business schools have adopted the concept of culture from anthropology, just as they have accepted and contributed to other behavioral science ideas. Like successful managers "on the ground," they have discovered that every company—certainly every big company—has its own, distinguishing culture. This culture concerns the aims of the company in the quality of its products, in how those are to be advertised and distributed, in what it hopes the public response to its products will be, and how the company will be perceived in the world at large. It also has to do with how it treats its employees and the way suggestions and new ideas are allowed to flow through the system.

The culture of one corporation differs interestingly from the culture of other corporations. Management consultants (like James O'Toole, who teaches in a business school, has an earned doctorate in anthropology, and writes extensively on corporate cultures) and managers (like Robert Galvin, chairman of Motorola) are acutely aware not only that corporate culture exists, but that employees, if given a voice, will become committed to the company and its culture rather than merely considering themselves to have a job there. A company culture that prizes employees not only for their labor but for their ideas creates a firm bond with them: people are happy to work at such a place. Moreover, whenever the public approves of a corporate culture, that company gains stature, its products gain favor, and its bottom line flourishes.

This is *not* merely an exercise in public relations. All employees and most customers easily see through the hype of PR. As voters, as employees, and especially as consumers, people resent being lied to.

In the late 1990s, the culture of the corporations that manufacture cigarets was publicly exposed as conscienceless and cynically manipulative. Their chief executive officers (CEOs) were not only initially suspected of having lied to Congress, but caught doing so on TV where everybody could watch. Their lawyers were faulted for stonewalling every effort to get at the facts. Their products were portrayed as at least as dangerous as those of drug dealers, and their managers were regarded as the sort of people who, in an earlier age, would have dealt in slaves but now grew far richer trafficking in lingering death for private profit. Although those perceptions may not have made very many people give up smoking—that inability *is* the characteristic nature of addiction, after all—they certainly did not improve the image of the companies or, one assumes, the self-respect of those who worked for them.

Unless it doesn't mind being perceived as purely predatory, it behooves every business to examine its products and their effects on its customers; it should also examine what it demands of its employees and how those demands affect the rest of its workers' lives. And because the collection of that sort of information is ethnography, it behooves every business to hire competent ethnographers to keep in touch with customers, employees, and the other companies with which it does business. To be effective, these ethnographers must be able to tell management, without fear of reprisals, how the company is viewed by its employees and by the public, and how its products are regarded. Good industrial anthropologists can then help the organization make appropriate adjustments that positively affect its image and its products before difficulties grow to be insurmountable.

If all companies would hire such specialists, and if the ethnographers were brave enough to be honest, government control agencies would have *far* less to do. If enough corporations do *not* do this, then in the not-too-distant future the public may demand that government begin *enforcing* the behavior standards set forth in corporate mission statements. Think of *that* as just one more "Attorney-Full-Employment-Act." Good industrial ethnographers are not only cheaper, they'll keep everybody happy and honest a lot earlier in the game.

Ethnography—understanding The Other as a step in understanding The Self—can thus be used to turn a profit. It is, in fact, already permeating some industries. Many others are probably not far behind. Good ethnography is not, however, good only for business. It is good for the general welfare of everyone. And if that isn't "good business," what is?

Chapter Twenty-One

Ethnography and Creativity
Art, Science, and Engineering

All societies need people to interpret, design, and build what is needed, to imagine other ways to live and act, and to create images of abstract ideas. All societies have people who do the things we call "art," "literature," "science," "mathematics," and "engineering." If we insist that our own achievements are the standards by which to judge all others, we will forego the chance to adapt their good ways into our culture and miss out on creativity of a major kind.

Every society needs people who understand how things work. Such people everywhere are creative—they can imagine alternatives, invent tools, and make representations or sounds that will please the gods or the ancestors for the simple reason that they please people. In the languages of industrial and post-industrial peoples, these creative individuals are called scientists, engineers, storytellers, artists, and prophets. But the languages of preindustrial societies may have no special terms at all for any of them.

We have a tendency to think that if people lack categorizing words for "art" or "engineering" or "religion," they must also lack the capacity for them. Not so, of course. Indeed, some of their ideas, when adapted to our own circumstances, can offer immense benefits to our own culture. This kind of adaptation may not be "original," but it *is* creative!

Originality, which we esteem so highly in fashion, art, and advertising, may just be a weird predilection of our own culture. We should remember two things about originality: first, like love, it usually occurs spontaneously and is not something you can make yourself be or do on demand. And second, most original ideas everywhere are terrible. Mercifully, most are also quickly forgotten. History is littered with abandoned original ideas and artifacts that didn't make it.

It is easy to confuse originality with creativity; self-styled poets and artists do it every day, as does the mother of the child rubbing its feces on the wall. But creativity is a social necessity: it is demanded every day from almost everybody, just to keep the culture going. It requires both a willingness and the ability to make things work even when they are not perfectly designed for their function. Creativity, from one valid point of view, is what culture is all about.

Creativity is also easy to confuse with art. "Art" is now a category of stuff and activities that can be taught in the schools, like spelling or geography (although funding may be denied by Philistine legislators who define art as irrelevant). Paradoxically, art is now also something that people can claim not to know anything about—or, even worse and almost as easily, everything about. As we specialize in our chosen fields, those of us who are not artists may mutter that we are "inadequately trained" and use that as an excuse to turn our backs on art—and on one of the major dimensions of creativity. For art, like ethnography, makes us see and understand everything in new ways.

The fact remains that people everywhere make and use representations to give meaning to what they value about their existences—through their carvings, their songs, their dances, their paintings, their theologies, and their cosmologies. That has created so many contextual meanings, and art now manifests them in so many ways for so many purposes, that even a committee of specialists could not hope to sort them out. But art is, in the final analysis, an intensely personal experience, and its evocative functions are not entirely eliminated by taking it out of its context.

If you are not privy to its meaning, you may wonder whether some particular work of art is "any good." Of course symbols work whether they are "any good" or not. And art critics will gladly tell you what "real" art is, but accepting their bombast risks depriving yourself of the capacity to experience it. To complicate things and render the *category* art essentially meaningless, *everything* now *claims* to be art: we have "the art of the deal" and "the art of the double-cross." Art has become a category without parameters; art is a way to package a product.

At this stage it is impossible to determine whether art or language is more debased. Which makes it more fruitful to talk about creativity.

One of the very best sources of creativity is ethnography, because that lets us know what Others have made and thought. Written ethnographies have usually dealt well with some of the creative areas of life. Folklorists have recorded stories from many places (although the process of reducing alien stories to mere print may leave out much of the context and therefore the drama). Decorations and sculptures from all over the world have been recorded in photographs and drawings—Picasso's encounter with African art changed his whole aesthetic.

The religious dogmas of many peoples have been faithfully recorded, and for all that these creeds are sometimes denigrated by unbelievers as "mere superstition," their axioms and logics and the moral codes that follow from them are available to those who wish to understand other ways of contemplating the ineffable.

People almost everywhere decorate their tools and weapons, and early anthropologists exhaustively studied these photogenic artifacts—huge collections of them are found in museums. But engineering and science have been short-changed, perhaps because most ethnographers lack the specialized training necessary to describe their alien evidence in "scientific" language and therefore ignore it altogether. Still, people everywhere *do* make houses, weapons, tools, and whatever else they need, and everywhere they know which physical principles will work and which won't, even though their society may lack any complex conceptualization of physics or design.

In ignoring this ethnographic material, in buying into the myth that describing alien efforts at craftsmanship and pragmatism requires a lot of specialist training and education, we lose a lot of illuminating detail. Tiv in the 1950s, for instance, built round houses. They got them round by driving a stake into the ground, looping a piece of (homemade) rope around it and putting a bare foot into the other end of the loop. Then, pulling the rope taut, they dragged that foot until the outline of the resulting circle was clear on the ground. Then they asked the clients whether this was big enough, exactly where the door should go (although all doors faced into the center of the ring of houses, that left ninety degrees of choice), and whether they wanted a drying platform above the fireplace in the middle of the circle. When all that had been decided, construction commenced. Great architecture it may not have been, but houses got built and everybody was pleased. It was good enough, and no one stayed homeless among the Tiv.

Everywhere people observe and try to predict the weather. They know about the seasons and the regularities in nature—often more than any Westerners except specialists. Ordinary Tiv know more about the moon and its cycles than anybody in the United States or Europe except astronomers. I learned it from them, then checked it out with experts when I got home. But if I try to explain the moon to my neighbors, some of them consider my views merely my opinion—which, by definition, is no better than their own opinion based on ignorance. They can afford their ignorance: the moon has no importance to them. But it was important to Tiv, who *always* knew what was happening with it.

People everywhere number and count. Even if higher mathematics may not be useful to them, arithmetic of some sort is functional. Some count in base-10 (as we do), others in base-6, or 12, 20 or whatever—the base doesn't matter, but counting is important. Tiv of the 1950s counted in base-20, using an elaborate system of gestures to duplicate and thereby reinforce and check the numbers as they spoke them. There were specific words for one, two, and three; but four was two-and-two. There were words for five, ten, and twenty. The word for six was "three-and-three"; seven was "five-and-two." Twenty-nine, translated literally, was "twenty-and-five-and-two-and-two." They had no trouble at all with the British idea that there were ten "tenth-pennies" (a denomination the British introduced when they made the coin) in a penny, twelve pennies in a shilling, and twenty shillings in a pound. I have seen them count into the hundreds; it may sound clumsy to us, but it served them well enough. Besides, "clumsy" is in the eye of the beholder: in French, ninety-nine is "four-twenties-and-ten-and-nine"—but that hasn't kept the French from adding significantly to the sciences.

The point is: you can't run a culture—*any* culture—without knowing something about the way things work. Your way may be narrow, and you might just learn something useful from other ways of looking at how they work. What many societies do indeed lack is any notion that their knowledge can be fitted together into some larger perspective called "science" and that the structures they design and the problems they solve are "engineering." Just so, it never occurs to them to call the figurines they carve or the designs they weave into cloth "art."

The creative disciplines (which *do* carefully delineate dance from music and belief, art from storytelling, and so forth) are the theoretical developments of some advanced culture, whether it be the ancient Chinese, pre-Islamic Arab, basic Mayan, or early Christian. Because you and I grew up with such categories, our perceptual universe is predicated upon them. But ours is not the only game in town. If we fail to look at what Others do, we may be overlooking a lot of sensible knowledge that might solve some problems in our own culture. For example, only in the last few decades have Westerners conceded the immediate pharmacological and medical potential in the knowledge and skills of the world's non-Western and preliterate societies.

For us, the immediacy of creativity tends to be lost in a maze of specialty disciplines. Art, science, engineering, and theology have each become fields so complex that a lot of training is required to master them—and so well organized that social rank becomes entrenched with certain specific ways of doing things.

Though art may have become a hollow category for many of us, creativity has never been more appreciated. We expect it from our scientists and demand it from our engineers; we reward it in our storytellers and dramatists, in our dancers and musicians and actors. But creativity is just as important for mechanics or executives—not to mention the people who keep our houses clean and in repair. And understanding how the world of The Other works will immeasurably improve your ability to make creative contributions to your own world.

Chapter Twenty-Two

Ethnography and Government

Laws work best when their makers recognize that the people who must live by them come from many different cultural groups and may therefore differ importantly in how they perceive the laws.

The two traditional purposes of government are to settle disputes among the citizens and to protect them from harm. In today's complex societies, however, governments have been handed a lot of other tasks—not because governments do them well but because there are no other institutions that can do them at all. Government and the family are "back-up" institutions—they are there when we have to handle new or difficult tasks before we get around to creating specialized institutions. They back up the whole society and the whole culture.

We have assigned to government the task of protecting us from those excesses of our culture which, if left uncontrolled, would ruin society or kill people. Culture can help people live better and more rewarding lives—but sometimes, some of its aspects can turn on the very people it is supposed to be helping. This fact was realized only in the 1950s, in books like Jules Henry's *Culture Against Man*.

Governments have, for example, stopped manufacturers from selling poisons and narcotics under the name of medicine (but cigaret sales are still legal); they have set up laboratories to test medicines and foods for public safety. Governments try to figure out what to do with people who have fallen through the cracks—who lack the know-how or the character to get or keep a job or who have become unemployed through no fault of their own. During the Great Depression of the early 1930s, when the suffering of working people throughout the world reached epidemic proportions, governments were forced to step in because no other help was at hand.

When they venture beyond their basic political tasks, governments may not do any of these things to everybody's satisfaction. They are damned if they interfere and damned if they don't; the argument about how much "government control" is too much is probably a permanent part of any democracy's culture. However, government will necessarily continue to be one of our major back-up institutions when other institutions are lacking, or fail. The trick, once government has stepped in, is to find a better nongovernmental way to do what is needed. But that's usually easier said than done. Because the problems brought on by the Great Depression were so severe, welfare grew enormously under the auspices of governments. We are still struggling with the results.

The creation of Social Security, also in the 1930s, was a reaction to immense society-wide problems about how to take care of increasing numbers of old people; now we live decades longer and still struggle with that adaptation.

In their early days, various forms of socialism, including communism, were seen as government responses to such pervasive problems. Today those responses are recognized as having taken on a life of their own and are widely discredited. However, as the family does for private woes, government remains the institution we turn to for (preliminary) solutions to wide-spread social problems.

The underlying difficulty is thus not so much with government itself as with the fact that we have found no alternative ways to achieve certain purposes. We realize that new kinds of problems will show up as the world gets ever more complex with more people, more technology, and more dangers, but we have a tendency to curse the government instead of addressing the issues.

Here and elsewhere, some rigid ideologues argue that governments should *never* attempt jobs for which society has no specialized institutions. They ignore the fact that when suffering and hunger affect large segments of a population, people may get desperate enough to take actions that make matters even worse. Remember the burning of Los Angeles and a score of other cities when civil rights was still a racial issue.

Society thus faces two moral questions: first, how many people must we lose before the government can step in and try to help? Second, and harder to answer, how do we foster new ways for doing jobs that government was never designed to do?

One place to look for alternatives, of course, is in the social laboratories we usually think of as Other Countries. For example, three problems that have vexed the United States for generations concern access to medicine, use of illegal drugs, and prolongation of dying. On all these subjects there have been promising innovations by numerous European societies. What stops us from looking at their answers and approaches? And what stops us from investigating how societies which are (or were) not nation-states handle such issues?

Elected officials, who are at the heart of all government functions, need accurate ethnographic information about the people they represent. It isn't very smart to say, "I'm one of them, so I know." Politicians, like the rest of us, have only limited cultural experience. They have to "go home" and ask questions and listen to the answers: adequate political representation requires a very specialized kind of ethnography. They also need information about the people who are affected by their laws (who may not be the same as those they represent).

The problem is made difficult because an official can neither ignore what people say they want, nor assume that what they ask for will actually solve their problems. And certainly no official can assume that all the persons in any cultural group will want the same thing.

Information feedback from the governed is an essential aspect of every administration that prides itself on providing what the majority of people vote for. Politicians' constituents call them up and gripe. Every problem that a complainant can describe clearly, the lawmaker may be able to do something about. A lot of things are wanted for selfish reasons—when the lawmaker provides them, Americans call it "pork." Often, however, constituents are unable to pinpoint the precise cause of their discomfort, sometimes because the culture has never before faced that particular problem. Yet people *still* demand that the government make their discomfort disappear. Knowing he cannot possibly scratch their itch, but knowing also that he'd better look as if he's really trying, the politician brings out smoke and mirrors to make things appear more difficult than they are. Wheels spin, words fly, red tape dresses things up and— Voilà!—it is clearly the opposition's fault that things have gotten this bad.

Note the irony: it is easier for politicians (and everybody else) to complicate things than to simplify them. Simplification takes more knowledge and *much* more creativity. Ethnographers who are consulted by government must become experts at simplification—at explaining alternatives to all that obstructive complication. There almost always arises a need for simplification after some basic cultural premise has been overlooked—and it is ethnography, after all, that illuminates cultural premises.

Lawmakers need ethnographic assistance in many contexts: What do people *mean* by what they are saying? (Perhaps more, perhaps less, than their words imply to Others.) What cultural premises lie behind their overt statements? Why are people not only uncomfortable, but unable to tell exactly *why* they are uncomfortable? What values and precepts are affected by proposed legislation, and how will they predispose the voters' response? Congress, state legislators, the courts, government agencies—all can only behave ethnocentrically and therefore oppressively when they lack accurate ethnographic information about citizens whose values and customs are different from their own.

Politicians sometimes reject ethnographic assistance for the wrong reasons—not only does it force them to re-examine their own behavior or their policies, but attitudinal change is even harder for politicians and diplomats than it is for you and me. They have been forced to subscribe to the myth that powerful people must be "consistent" as a means of demonstrating that they "stand for something." Any scientist can say "I was wrong there," and go on with the business of figuring out how the universe works. But politicians are under a very different kind of magnifying glass: they are loath to admit error because they think it will cost them credibility. That is just one of the reasons why so many of us, realizing that every human must err sometimes, have so much trouble trusting politicians.

The fact remains: ethnography is no longer something we can afford to leave to anthropologists. The more of us, including those in government, who learn to ask good questions *and listen to the answers*, the better off we all will be.

Chapter Twenty-Three

The Internet
Non-Lineal Ethnography

When ethnographic information enters the Internet, the new context creates a non-lineal ethnography. There, the viewpoints and premises that have traditionally given meaning to ethnographic facts are lost. The uses of the information in the new context seem utterly unpredictable. With ethnography thus escaping its refuge in anthropology, people can use its data and theories in the service of any purpose whatsoever.

With tourism and international trade prospering, there are no longer any undiscovered parts of the world. Today, "strange" people include our neighbors—and even ourselves: it may just be that our own culture (however you may want to define, limit, or extend *that*) is the weirdest one of all.

The Information Age ushers us into a new cultural era—one that includes a new phase in ethnography. Information finds itself in a totally new context. I discovered that fact when I put my twenty or so articles and several books about the Tiv on a single CD-ROM. All the information on any topic could now be aligned, regardless of the context in which I had originally written it. There was no way in which I could control the new context. Here, before my eyes, was the new non-lineal ethnography: interactive, with the Reader in control.

We have entered a new kind of context for all information, not just for ethnographic information.

Change of a similar sort has occurred before as knowledge grew. It happened, for example, each time writing was invented someplace. Writing creates a new kind of memory. It also creates the basis for new class-divisions: the literate and the illiterate. This also happened with geographical knowledge: when information on the earth's physical features, climates, and resources was first being collected systematically, it became the property of royalty and of armies—you could win battles if you knew the geography. In Columbus's day, ordinary people were not allowed to own maps. As a bona fide sea captain, Columbus did have them, but for unauthorized people to own maps was a serious offense. And the same thing happened with meteorology: as late as World War II, weather reports were not printed or broadcast in either Europe or the United States because letting foreigners know what your weather was or would be was "giving comfort to the enemy."

Today our secrets concern industrial processes, military hardware, and personal information like credit card numbers. Businesses must keep competitors from stealing their know-how. Governments still have secrets and still sponsor "intelligence" groups to discover what other governments are keeping from them. Individually we are increasingly concerned that information about ourselves is being exposed on the Internet. New ideas about privacy are being proposed as we ask anew, "What *is* a secret—and why *should* it be secret?"

Information is power. Again, consider writing. The literate *always* become more powerful than the illiterate, although at various times in history, rulers have reduced literate people to be subservient to themselves or turned them into a specialist-class, even into slaves. In the long run, however, such attempts to control information were not successful. You can't control literacy without totalitarianism—and in the long run, totalitarianism fails against any system that adapts more rapidly by allowing information to flow more freely!

The typewriter changed social structures everywhere. The earliest typists were men, because the typewriter was a machine and running a machine was defined as men's work. But as soon as typing came to be seen as a service, it turned into women's work. Learning to type did indeed give women a new way to be self-supporting—and some of them could now escape whatever miserable lot they found themselves in. But it also kept women one-down in status. Today, with computer literacy being a sign of administrative competence, men are no longer ashamed to admit they can type—as they actually were as recently as the 1970s. Men who have grown up using a keyboard may well be unable to figure out why this skill was once thought effeminate. But it was; otherwise why did so many men—and some powerful women—so blatantly advertise the fact that they could not type?

The mimeograph, too, played an important part in culture change. It was a device that preceded the photocopying machine. You had to type a "stencil" which was a sort of soft plastic sheet that typewriter keys could pierce—or at least bruise enough that ink would seep through. You then spread the stencil over an inked drum, after which you rolled sheets of paper across the drum by turning a crank. The ink seeping through the holes in the stencil made an impression on the sheet of paper.

You may well be grateful that this contraption was replaced before you had to deal with it—but do realize that the mimeograph was an early victory in the personalization and democratization of publishing. Soviet authorities in Communist Russia realized that the mimeograph made it possible to circulate ideas without their permission, and therefore threatened their authority. Consequently they tried to control its use—as they had the typewriter and later the computer. Their totalitarian attempts to regulate the flow of information—

even though they were never totally successful—slowed their society's techno-logical evolution enough to guarantee their regime's eventual fall.

It is hard to remember today what kinds of information had to be kept secret in former centuries—or even decades. But there is a second point: the Information Age has also given us new ways to lie. Many animals lie (for all that some people, ignoring the facts of ethology, may have told you that only human beings lie; they say such things in order to preserve myths about inno-cence in the "natural" world). But given the new technology, human beings can now lie on a broader scale than ever before. The new euphemism for lies is "misinformation," and today it is up to *you* to figure out how to tell it from fac-tual information. And that requires some education.

But the revolution doesn't stop there; it directly affects ethnography. It is now possible to get all the information ever recorded about any people into a single source on the Internet, or onto some device like a CD-ROM (or what-ever even-more-efficient technology replaces it). Constantly evolving and improving technology allows us now to discover and compare what different observers have said about that society at various times in its history.

A quick review will get all this into perspective. With the growth of cul-tural anthropology in the last decades of the 1800s, ethnography was turned to a new use—providing data for social and behavioral science theory. People with exotic lifeways became the focus of attention—something they had seldom or never been in the old travel books. The desire of social scientists to compare cultures fed the urge to "get it right" and "get it all." Whole libraries of ethno-graphic accounts sprang up—most, but not all, written by professional anthro-pologists.

Just as ethnography found a home in anthropology in the late 1800s, so it has now, a century later, grown secure enough to escape that refuge. Ethnog-raphy has become a way to explain ethnic differences—and has taken on a life of its own. Our universities run ethnic studies programs, usually about a spe-cific group; they also organize multi-cultural or "diversity" programs to explain and compare the history, literature, and other achievements of many populations. Ideally they also show how the successes and adaptations of each group are aligned with the achievements of other human beings. They are tak-ing the ethnocentrism out of history. Let us hope that they'll be able to do so without establishing a new ethnocentrism of their own.

We are witnessing the creation of a new reality in which some parts of culture are shared by all human beings while other parts are shared only by people with common interests. This has always been true—but now we can see it on a global scale. Ethnic groups have become common interest groups, some with more political clout than others.

Culture remains humanity's unique method for adapting to its environ-ments. But fieldworkers will have to figure out how to study new global con-texts of culture and people's new purposes. Is everybody becoming multicul-tural? We think it more likely that only the educated will—implying yet another sort of class-distinction, but one which you can do something about. Will there be whole new groups who are disadvantaged because they cannot participate? Probably. Will you be among them? If you have read this far and understood us, probably not.

This chapter asks a lot of questions without giving hard answers. But one thing we are sure of: ethnography—systematically asking strangers about themselves—is the best way to get answers. It just may be the only way. And that means that ethnography lies at the heart of the communications revolution.

Storing information in computers will as inevitably usher in new problems as the introduction of libraries did. In a computer, the meaning of the single unit of information is no longer stored as human language—it is stored in ones and zeroes, the mathematical symbols in base-2. Unless we have access to the code for turning it back into human language or the mathematics that accompany language, that knowledge exists essentially without context. At the very least, it is a new context—a new kind of culture. The computer stores culture just as books do, but with far greater efficiency—and far more skill is needed to "retrieve" it.

Anthropology has long prided itself on being the science of meaning, but meaning is contextual. What happens to ethnographic information now that context has been ripped away (as, earlier, colonialism was)? Obviously both the information and some sort of context still exist, but the computer environment puts a specific mark on it. "Facts" or bits of data may be juxtaposed by the computer, but they are *not* connected unless human beings make a special effort to create that connection—the context.

Once you reduce a "fact" to a "datum" that you can retrieve electronically, it requires special effort and know-how to restore it to a real-world context. Ethnographic context has traditionally meant the fact's original, real-world, human setting. Strip that away, and the "fact" you have left is almost meaningless. What does 01111101010100 mean?

But when you ask that question, you find yourself face to face with the fact that *no* symbol has ever meant anything except what somebody decided it meant. In language, those decided meanings can be organized into "cultures." But here's an odd fact: in the computer, such a level of organization is far more difficult to achieve, in spite of the fact that the computer can do all sorts of things that ordinary language finds difficult or impossible.

Words however—including words in foreign languages that you haven't learned yet—carry more meaning for people than strings of zeroes and ones do. For all that you can say that a binary code is just another language, the processes of translation have been altered. Culture contains more meanings than words. "A culture" is a set of meanings derived from beliefs and juxtapositions of bits of information. What happens to "a culture" in the binary language of the computer?

We have said repeatedly, in many ways, that all ideas have many interpretations. The number of possible interpretations increases with the distance between symbol and perceived reality (however culture-bound). That number begins to approach infinity when more-or-less-contextless information is encoded in computers. *Anybody* can make an interpretation, and yours can be said to be as good as mine. Where is "the culture" in *that* situation?

Yet now more than ever, ideas remain a principal part of the armamentarium by which our species survives. Since a thing, a fact, can have so many meanings attached to it that each person becomes an untrammeled arbiter of meaning, what purposes—old or new—can ethnographic "data" be made to serve? Facts stripped of their context are scary; we don't know where they will lead us. But we better not get too scared—we have a lot of stuff to figure out.

It is still too early to tell just where such "context-challenged facts" will take us. However, it is *not* too early to predict that it's going to be a wild ride. Ethnography can now be allowed to flow into a not-yet-established bank of more-or-less "total" information about the human species (we visualize some cultural equivalent of the genome project, which catalogs all human genes) to be used by anybody.

For anything.

As the idea of culture has already done, ethnography is slipping into the hands of Everyman. Anthropologists may resent losing control of it, but that too will have exactly *no* effect. The choreography of culture change is out of our hands—it always was. But we have never had such a fine opportunity to begin *not* to control it, but to *understand* it!

We need a lot of thought and a lot of information about all this. Will the Internet help us expand our options and our range of culture? Will it help us to understand people and the way they interact with one another? It could, but it could also be overwhelmed by other efforts to turn the ultimate technology for reuniting humanity into a means for exploiting it with more ruthless efficiency.

We are witness to the birth of a new stage in cultural evolution. The idea that all of recorded human experience can be accessed and used for *anyone's* idiosyncratic purpose is exciting on a number of levels, not all of them attractive. We do, indeed, live in interesting times. And not the least interesting thing about them is that all human knowledge is being collected and encoded, while meaning and context are either being ignored or else transformed into art that will alter, inform, and change . . . everything.

Welcome to the Third Millennium.

Part IV

The Curse of Ethnocentrism

At least two intellectual disorders beset multi-ethnic societies (which today means most societies) and international relationships. The first and oldest is ethnocentrism: the belief that one's own culture sets the standard against which all others are to be judged.

The second, tempocentrism, is ethnocentrism about a time period—the belief that our own time (particularly the golden age of our childhood and early youth) is the standard against which all history and all policies are to be judged. Tempocentrism gets virulent when culture changes rapidly.

Ethnography is the best inoculating serum so far known against these two disorders. It is, indeed, the only one to get at the basis of the problem rather than merely dealing with the symptoms.

Chapter Twenty-Four

Ethnocentrism in a Culture with Many Lifestyles

As societies get larger and culture becomes more complex, people's options increase and their responsibilities change. Choosing wisely is sometimes experienced as a heavy responsibility—especially when we become aware that our choices not only determine our own fates, but also affect other people. If we make ethnocentric choices, we cheat ourselves of the opportunity to widen our horizons and reach our potential. We also create social problems. Ethnocentrism is, thus, the secret spoiler of both individual lives and complex, multi-ethnic cultures.

Our themes in this book have been: (1) expanding your options leads to a more rewarding life, and (2) learning some ethnography, as a part of a broad general education, is the best way yet found to expand them.

However, there is a flip side. First, you have to live with your choices. Then also, you have to live with people who have made other choices.

The concept of ethnocentrism is broad. Democracy is a form of government that tries to get all views expressed openly so that people can choose among them. It is, of course, plagued by the fact that people (including politicians) perceive the ideas of others as evil "opposites" of what they consider their own virtues. We can perhaps learn to live with that—we can certainly learn not to be taken in by it.

In a complex society with lots of choices, the cultural distances between neighbors can grow into ravines. Almost *everybody* you deal with is a stranger—that *is*, after all, the logical end-product of a world that allows so many choices and so much personal fulfillment.

There is an important point here: living successfully with the kind of culture we are now faced with absolutely *demands* that we expand our capacity to see other viewpoints—and thus reduce the random noise created by all those culture gaps.

How, the question goes, do you conduct yourself in a cultural arena in which your field of choice is so wide that you have to reject most of the options just to determine your own identity, your own lifestyle? How can you achieve justice in a society in which flatly rejecting the views of others has become a common way to protect yourself from the ravages of doubt?

The ethnographic attitude has become a social necessity. It can get you through the hodgepodge of alternatives embraced by the people with whom you share your life space but not any great amount of your lifestyle. The problem for social scientists is a variation on the same question: how do people become aware of, understand, honor—and study—what is obviously their common culture at the same time that they allow for separate lifestyles?

How do we help each other? How do we help people who are faced with too many choices? Or people for whom real alternatives have been closed off? We all know, but sometimes prefer to forget, that some ethnic groups have historically been shut out of the mainstream of cultural growth and opportunity—racism is the most obvious but not the only example. Whole categories of people—like women—have often been restricted to too narrow a sphere, regardless of their talents.

Remember this: whenever *anybody* is not allowed to become what he or she has the brains, brawn, and guts to become, all of us are cheated because the growth of culture has been curtailed.

If you yourself cannot recognize restrictions on yourself, you will drown in purposelessness. And if "they" restrict you, you have to learn to face them down—even risk making the world *safe* for facing them down—or else drop out.

An awareness of ethnography lets each of us spell out the options by telling us what "Others" around the world, and down the street, have already worked out.

Because ethnocentrism is built into most cultures, the ethnographic attitude becomes a major tool. It affords you space to stand outside your usual experience—a place to wedge your lever as you try to make a difference.

The more options your culture provides, the more you need ethnographic skills. With every decision you make, you create not only your career, but your lifestyle—your own "idioculture"—your private version of whatever culture you share with the people around you. In that sense, your adult culture becomes your personal creation as well as your personal responsibility. And in the process, you give a tone to whatever culture you share with everybody else.

Seen against that backdrop, ethnography does indeed become an irreplaceable tool to help you put your personal culture together and link it with the personal cultures of other people.

To summarize: in small-scale cultures that offer a comparatively narrow band of options, people become differentiated on the basis of their unique abilities and experiences. They usually do not, however, grow alien to one another. Ethnocentrism, in their societies, operates against clearly recognizable outsiders. In complex societies, many of those outsiders are on the inside. Complex culture—and the way we have to use it—makes us strangers to one another. Is all this true for every complex society? Is it true in France, in Russia, in China, in Argentina, in Bangladesh? *Must* it be true?

Cultural complexity enriches our lives by offering us choices so that we can become more truly ourselves. But that very process makes us strangers to one another—and we human beings distrust strangers, often for good reason.

Chapter Twenty-Five

Ethnocentrism in a Shrinking World

Almost everybody nowadays partakes of several cultures. When world-wide communication became instantaneous and travel was democratized, a global culture developed. Of course this can never create total uniformity because its range (like that of any other cultures) is narrow. Meanwhile the number of new, small-scale cultures which are based neither on geography nor ethnicity is also increasing, and ethnocentrism, the most dangerous trap in international relations, grows more subtle.

As increasing numbers of us travel as tourists and do business abroad, more of us encounter people and conditions that are strange to us. Corporations like Coca-Cola, Hilton Hotels, KFC, Royal Dutch Shell, Levi Strauss, McDonalds, Sony, Toyota, and Visa have all found it profitable to present us with the familiar wherever we go. That kind of standardization is the basis of a global culture. While the Internet speeds up this development, people as strange to us as any we've met in Outer Faraway have moved within a few blocks of our homes.

It soon becomes evident that many of today's young cultures have no territorial reference. Born free of geography, they can take many forms—forms that allow them to insert themselves into almost any society in such a way that people fail to sense any discontinuity.

The development of global culture became apparent several decades ago with the worldwide appetite for American movies. It is older than that, but seems not to have been noticed until then. At first it was disdained as the "Hollywood influence." Not that all movies are made in Hollywood, of course, but they do offer an excellent example of the way global culture and local cultures fit together. Many nations support a film industry. One of the largest is India's, although few Indian pictures are exported to the West. Language may be one factor why this is so, although it is fairly easy to dub an English language ver-

96

sion. A more telling reason is the content that derives from local cultures. Often their symbolism and underlying value-assumptions, though powerful and compellingly presented, are so alien as to be wasted on outsiders who can approach the film only through their own culture—global culture has nothing to say about the situation. Consequently and in general, the output of alien nations' film industries—like those of Japan, Russia, and the Netherlands— tends to be labeled "art" film in the United States and is shown only to tiny audiences in scruffy theaters.

Global culture does not cover very many aspects of human life; it leaves plenty of room for traditional cultures as well as the new ones based on shared interest.

Airport and hotel culture, for example, is international. A hotel in Amsterdam, Bangkok, or Cuzco is a lot like a hotel in Denver or Toronto or Singapore. Weather-forecasting culture is also pretty much the same the world over—after all, weather is a global phenomenon. So, of course, are politics and economics and TV's news and entertainment.

News-hour culture is everywhere. During the Desert Storm War, the president of Turkey heard the president of the United States say in a live interview on CNN that he was going to telephone the president of Turkey just as soon as he finished talking to the reporter. The Turkish president rushed to his office so he could answer his telephone when the call came. He got there in time.

This is an important point: CNN covers the world. However, CNN is produced mainly by Americans and necessarily puts their spin on what it reports. When people from other places see that spin, they label it "American." If they disagree with it they'll accuse not CNN but "the Americans" of being pushy, power-mad, and meddlesome. There are two factors at work here: American ethnocentrism and the ethnocentrism of the viewers. CNN *is* ethnocentric—it more-or-less-unconsciously focuses on "American" concerns and values. Just so, the BBC carries British values (although BBC International hires enough natives of their broadcasts' target countries to minimize this tendency), and Deutsche Welle carries German values. It would take a lot of time to watch them all to allow the various ethnocentrisms to cancel each other out.

It is *very* difficult for reporters and editors (or anybody else) to detect ethnocentrism in themselves. And it is even more difficult to keep that ethnocentrism from interfering with the smooth operation of global culture. Recognizing this, nations and corporations try to control more obvious and obnoxious expressions of ethnocentrism, but that does not eliminate such feelings within individuals. Repression simply forces people to be more subtle about their prejudices; it makes ethnocentrism more difficult to recognize.

Ethnocentrism, once confused with patriotism but now extended to all jingoisms and chauvinisms, has been under the gun of late, at least in the developed world. Thanks to half a century of the memory of the Holocaust and of watching ethnic conflicts on television, the term now calls up the Ku Klux Klan or the Neo-Nazis, Serbian concentration camps and Hutu-Tutsi genocide. So if your peers think you ethnocentric today, it means they see you as not merely prejudiced by your parent culture, but as hopelessly provincial. Caught out this way, ethnocentrism may go underground—we are not aware of it until our "friends" suddenly start to hate us. When our own ethnocentrism has to be pointed out to us, we tend to regard that as an unjustified condemnation of our values rather than as criticism of our methods of communication. Consequently, ethnocentrism remains a major problem in world affairs. No one knows how much time the representatives of nation-states spend talking *past* instead of *to* each other.

Diplomats occupy a niche similar to ethnographic fieldworkers in this sense: first they have to figure out what people on the other side are trying to tell them, then they must discuss it with them to make sure that they have understood each other correctly. Diplomats especially are therefore in constant need of ethnographic advice—what are the Russians (or the Chinese or the Greeks or the Brits) really saying when they tell us something that we think we already understand? There have always been glitches in the way ideas are translated from one language to another. The values of any people seem so obvious to themselves that they cannot fathom how anyone could mean anything else by those words and hence understand the situation differently.

The crucial question is this: what North American ideas keep North Americans from *hearing* clearly what the Chinese are saying? One reason that misunderstanding between these peoples is so common may be their profoundly different attitudes toward authority and power. American and Canadian views assume that all human beings have the capacity to adjust and organize their own actions; we must therefore give each person both the power to do so and good reasons for doing it in prosocial ways. The Chinese view, insofar as we can fathom it, assumes that only centralized authorities have access to all the information necessary to make decisions that benefit everyone; it therefore seems sensible to reserve power for those who understand its limits and its uses—and by extension to insist that individuals bow to authority in matters about which they, by definition, have inadequate knowledge. As a result, the two sides fail to communicate even when they use the same words and believe they are in accord.

Language itself has taken on a global tone; English has emerged as the vernacular of global culture without replacing other tongues for other kinds of cultures or for other purposes. In medieval times, Latin was the language of scholarship throughout the Western world (as, in some other regions, Arabic and Sanskrit served such purposes). In the nineteenth and early twentieth centuries, French was the language of diplomacy; knowing French was a sign that you were an educated cosmopolitan. Since the Second World War, English—the language of science and technology—has become the world's *lingua franca* (which is a Latin term for French). If you've ever watched world news, you know that many people in remote parts of the world understand English well enough to get the message and can speak at least a few halting but comprehensible words to a reporter.

Global culture, like every other type, demands and creates a common set of values and assumptions. What we may be witnessing here (fear and joy are both highly appropriate) is technology reinforcing our biological similarities and overcoming our cultural differences—and thereby bringing the human species together under a single, infinitely customizable (if limited) culture.

But that new global culture is *not* now swamping all other cultures, and it never will. It is too highly specialized. Even as it demands that we invent new traits faster than was ever necessary or possible before, and though it demands that we ask a lot of questions no one has ever asked before, it covers only a few aspects of human life.

Let us emphasize this fact: The rise of a global culture does *not* mean the end of cultural diversity. It means, rather, that interest groups can form cross-culturally. People with different local cultures who are concerned with the same subjects can form communities of interest. The Internet has vastly speeded up this process. Interest groups need not be ethnocentric, but their members may be horribly so—in everything except that specific shared concern. The flow and mix of ethnocentrism—of misunderstood viewpoints—gets more complex daily.

Yet, even as airports reduce travelers' stress by presenting a worldwide sameness, people do still "go home." They can leave all that global culture behind because it is relevant to only a few aspects of their lives. Once again the meaning of "home" is changing: where the Industrial Revolution turned it into a place people had to leave to "go to work," today home is becoming a refuge against global culture—and from political culture and corporate culture and all those other cultures that vie for our attention.

Everybody can now be said to have access to many special-purpose cultures. Everybody lives in many contexts—and in each of them some small portion of the culture of each member is expressed. Is there such a thing as "a culture" anywhere any more? Was there ever? Or was that just a "hypothetical construct," something anthropologists made up for their own convenience?

The culture we live in is now so complex and so abstract that it forces our special-interest cultures to be not merely visible but obvious. As the complexity of culture keeps increasing, lifestyles proliferate in response, and individual responsibility for one's own lifestyle becomes more evident.

There is an immense opportunity for ethnography here! All we have to do is figure out, first, how to collect and document information on how ethnicity creeps into our interaction, and then how to use such data. The two of us are convinced that this opportunity will engage and employ a lot of people, particularly ethnographers, in the twenty-first century.

Chapter Twenty-Six

Tempocentrism and the Future

What people hope will happen and what they fear will happen can easily be made part of every ethnographic study—all you have to do is ask and listen. Doing that can open windows on the future as people work to bring about their hopes and avoid their fears.

Tomorrow is already here—just as the past is still here. However, we have to learn to understand both. Historians know well that the way we see the past of our own society and our own culture may be very different from the ways people who lived in that past saw it. Just so, the future we see today is different from the way people who live there will see it. Being unaware of the differences is an example of tempocentrism, that variety of ethnocentrism which uses today's culture as the standard for judging and understanding cultures of the past or future.

Ethnography provides one of the few sensible ways to discover what tomorrow's possibilities may be—the only one if you disregard science fiction. It cannot tell you what specific forms tomorrow will take, but it can indicate the range within which the next stages of growth will occur. Certainly there will be surprises: no ethnographer can predict exactly what specific events tomorrow will actually come up with.

Nevertheless, people *do* have ideas both about what they hope will happen and what they are afraid will happen, and they'll readily share them with you. Such hopes and fears can easily be made part of any ethnographic record: all you have to do is ask—and then listen carefully and without prejudgments to the answers. In fact, however, the ethnographic record almost never covers people's perceptions of the future. We encourage you to help change that.[1]

Almost everyone today looks to the future. All of us hope for something better than the worst we can imagine, for most of us have a pretty good idea of

100

how *bad* it can get, even if we don't agree on what constitutes the worst. Indeed, imagining the worst—sometimes called *dys*topias—has become a standard exercise in fiction and in movies. What is truly diagnostic of our age, however, is that we have so few credible *u*topias,[2] scenarios and descriptions of how *good* it can get. That oddity may identify a potentially lethal disparity between our hopes for the future and our fears of it.

Because people can think only with and within the terms and cultural premises they already know, their expected futures tend to resemble either nicer or nastier versions of today. This is a serious trap for those futurists who put their faith in projecting present trends: look at the futuristic movies made before the microchip was invented to discover how far off-base that can get you. Another trap is the assumption, common among prognosticators and science fiction writers alike, that no matter how much technology changes, human character stays constant. In point of fact, no one whose finger is on the trigger of a nuclear device can be equivalent in anything except DNA to a person whose finger is on the trigger of a crossbow. The main reason why immigrants and their American-born children are so often mutually alienated is not the technology each has grown up with, but the differing social systems that incorporate those technologies and (vastly more important!) the ideas and values surrounding their use.

As the tide of social and cultural change rises, people hope the world they know and prize will not be swept away. But they know it *could* be, and they fear it *will* be, because all of the old worlds *have* been. People necessarily define their best- and worst-case scenarios in terms of their old culture, much as we discuss inflation in terms of the value of our money at some period in our past.

When you ask "what are the best things that might happen?" and then "what are the worst?", listen to what people tell you. You will be able to detect what they believe to be the strongest or most desirable aspects of their current culture, and which are its most vulnerable or shameful points; what they cherish and want to protect; what they hate and want to get rid of.

When you then ask what is most *likely* to happen, people reveal the compromises they are willing to make with their hopes and what battles they are willing to fight to make sure their fears will not be realized. Here you run into what social scientists call the "self-fulfilling prophecy," for if people think that such-and-such is probable and if they can live with that, it is more likely to come about simply because they won't fight it when it starts to happen. Consciously or not, they'll help bring it about.

Hints of both the past and the prospects of a culture—its history and its future—are thus found within it. Both will, of course, be tweaked a little to fit the problems and parameters of a forthcoming present.

Our point here should be unambiguous: If you but ask, you can zero in on the problems that are bothering people. Up to a point, what people want to happen may actually come about because they work hard to bring it about. What they fear and work against may actually be avoided. Can you ask for better odds of any future?

Tomorrow has indeed arrived, as yesterday you knew it would. And it turns out that ethnography is not only a tool to control the ravages of ethnocentrism and tempocentrism, but a mechanism for taming (at least to some degree) the cultural processes going on around you. It is an awesome instrument for planning.

Best of all: properly used, ethnography will improve the quality of your own life today and tomorrow.

Notes

[1] The leader in what he calls "the ethnography of the future" has been Robert Textor. For examples, see his *A Handbook of Ethnographic Futures Research*, 3d edition (Stanford University School of Education and Department of Anthropology, 1980). A fine later example is J. A. English-Lueck, *Chinese Intellectuals on the World Frontier: Blazing the Black Path*, (Westport, CT: Bergin & Garvey, 1997).

[2] The original literary piece was Thomas More's *Utopia*, first published in Latin in 1516 and translated into English in 1551. His word means "nowhere" in Greek. It is often confused with Eutopia, which means "good place" in Greek. Dystopia is Latin for "bad" plus Greek for "place." A better word would be cacotopia (from the Greek, *kakos*, meaning "bad") which has two advantages: it sounds much worse than dystopia and it is all Greek.

Index